Primary Sources
Research findings in primary geography

edited by Stephen Scoffham

THE GEOGRAPHICAL ASSOCIATION

© The Geographical Association, 1998

ISBN 1 899085 51 3
First published 1998
Impression number 10 9 8 7 6 5 4 3 2 1
Year 2001 2000 1999 1998

Frontispiece photograph: Chris Garnett

Published by the Geographical Association, 160 Solly
Street, Sheffield S1 4BF. The Geographical Association is a
registered charity: no 313129.

The Publications Officer of the GA would be happy to
hear from other potential authors who have ideas for
geography books. You may contact the Officer via the GA
at the address above. The views expressed in this
publication are those of the authors and do not
necessarily represent those of the Geographical
Association.

Edited by Rose Pipes
Designed by Ledgard Jepson Limited
Printed and bound in England by the Thanet Press

Contents

Photo: Wendy Morgan

Introduction

How do children learn geography? What difficulties do they have in understanding the world around them? And are some methods of teaching more effective than others? These are key questions which anyone with an interest in geographical education needs to consider.

The intention of this book is to supply some answers. It was inspired by the conferences on primary geography held at Charney Manor in March 1995 and 1997 and seeks to bring research findings to a wider audience. A key theme throughout is that children's learning is affected by misconceptions. Many infants, for example, believe that their physical surroundings have been created by people rather than natural forces. We need to take these misconceptions into account if we are to develop children's ideas successfully, and to recognise that teaching is not just a matter of common sense.

Each contribution to this book has been written from a particular perspective. Some summarise specific research studies, others describe on-going projects or bring together key findings from recent publications. What they have in common is that they have direct implications for classroom teachers and curriculum planners. There is also an underlying concern for child development, though the authors do not adhere to any particular theory of learning.

The research reported here sets out a powerful and convincing case for geography. Not only does geography develop the thinking and learning skills that are essential in the modern world, it also contributes to children's emotional and spiritual development. Furthermore, children as young as three- and four-years old appear to be able to handle basic geographical concepts. Their sense of involvement and attachment to places, their concern for the environment and their ideas about different people and cultures all reach back to early childhood. We do them a serious disservice if we underestimate their potential and marginalise geography in the early years of education.

Currently, there is a wide-ranging discussion about the nature of geography and its place in the school curriculum. It is to be hoped that this book will help to ensure that the agenda for the future is based on evidence rather than anecdote or ideology, and that all who read it will engage in the debate. In particular, there is a need to think about research and its relationship to policy and practice, and to seek revisions to the primary geography curriculum that will meet the needs of children in the twenty-first century.

Stephen Scoffham

Primary Geography for the 21st Century

Steve Watts

As we approach the end of this millennium it is unclear how geography will form part of the primary curriculum at the start of the next. Yet there are powerful reasons, supported by a growing body of research, for introducing children to geography from the earliest age.

The future of primary geography

What will happen to primary geography in the new millennium? While we cannot be certain, what seems sure is that curriculum change, such a feature of the 1990s, is likely to continue unabated in the future. There is already a published timetable for revising the present Orders. Advice will need to be offered to the Secretary of State by April 1998 and working groups appointed by September 1998 if a new curriculum is to be implemented in the year 2000.

In addition the Qualifications and Curriculum Authority (QCA) is undertaking a wide-ranging review of the curriculum. Estelle Morris, Parliamentary Under Secretary of State for Education, has identified a number of principles that will underpin the debate:

- an overriding priority for higher standards of numeracy and literacy
- the need for an exciting, varied, forward-looking curriculum
- continuity and stability
- the need to look at the curriculum as a whole
- the need to look at the curriculum from the perspective of children and their stage of development
- collaboration with interested parties

It is to be hoped that this review will provide an opportunity to learn from past mistakes. The rationale for the original (1991) and revised (1995) Orders was never made sufficiently clear. This has made interpretation difficult and left teachers uncertain about what is expected. The structure for any future curriculum will need to be much more explicit.

There are many reasons for optimism about geography's future: we know, for instance, that subscriptions to *Primary Geographer* keep growing indicating the popularity of the subject in schools. We also know, from the growing body of research, that there are powerful reasons for introducing children to geography at an early age: the subject is uniquely placed to equip children with perspectives and understanding which will help them understand their place in the world, care for the environment and accept the responsibilities of citizenship.

Nevertheless, as Gerber and Lidstone (1996) warn us, complacency is dangerous:

> Geographical education cannot sit back and relax as the world progresses. Those people who profess to be geographical educators must recognise that their future is not guaranteed.'
> *Gerber and Lidstone, 1996, p.10*

It is for this reason that the unique attributes of the subject (see Figures 1 and 2) need to be broadcast as widely as possible.

Primary geography research

There is a growing body of research evidence about how children acquire their knowledge and understanding of the world and it is to be hoped that any future changes to the geography curriculum will be informed by this. It is well established, for example, that basic geographical notions develop at a very early age. Given suitable circumstances children as young as three and four can follow a route and describe different landmarks. By the time they come to school, many have developed ideas about other countries and places they have never visited.

Research findings also show that some ideas, particularly those to do with physical geography, are conceptually difficult and present a challenge even to upper juniors. Similarly, the technical language and vocabulary used by geographers presents problems for many children (see pages 20-21): they may be able to repeat the words but careful questioning often reveals that they understand very little about their meaning.

In the past, the impact of research findings on classroom practice and policy makers was slight. In 1988, Lidstone pointed out that:

> Research in geographical education does not seem to have been very well received by the teaching community nor does it seem to have had a great influence on policy makers.
> *Lidstone, 1988, p.282*

Today there is a growing trend for teachers to work alongside researchers in collaborative ventures. This enables practitioners to bring their expertise and perspectives to bear in a much more meaningful way. Small-scale studies, often conducted by students as part of their course work, have further added to our understanding. The Teacher Training Agency (TTA) and Schools Curriculum Assessment Authority (SCAA) have both invited teachers and educators to carry out school-based research. In a cooperative climate such as this, perhaps the link between research, policy and practice will at last be taken seriously.

References

Bridge, C. (1997) *Millennium Geography*. Paper for Geographical Association.

Gerber, R. and Lidstone, J. (1996) *Developments and Directions in Geographical Education*. Channel View.

Lidstone, J. (1988) 'Research in geographical education' in Gerber, R. (ed) *Developing Skills in Geographical Education*. IGUCGE and Jacaranda.

Morris, E. (1997) Address to SCAA conference 'Developing the Primary School Curriculum'.

Ten Key Contributions

- Geography is concerned with interpreting the human and physical forces that shape the Earth

- Geography provides mapwork skills and knowledge of the world map, both necessary to personal wayfinding and the location of world events and issues

- Geography studies the cycles, patterns and processes of the natural world

- Geography examines the processes which determine the interconnectedness of the contemporary world

- Geography explores the diversity of cultures and nations

- Geography highlights environmental change, the finite nature of resources and issues of sustainability from the local to the global (Agenda 21)

- Geography fieldwork actively explores rural and urban environments

- Geographical enquiry encourages the formation of opinions and the development of citizenship through explorations of the interaction of people in communities, their sense of place and awareness of responsibility for the environment

- Geography increasingly depends on information technology for the collection and analysis of data, communication of findings and contribution to the common store of information which enriches global understanding

- Geography works across time and scale as it seeks to interpret the present and raise awareness of trends for the next century

Figure 1. How geography contributes to the primary school curriculum (after Bridge, 1997)

Figure 2. What will geography do for me?

Photo: Chris Garnett

Children as Mapmakers

Simon Catling

Research conducted by the author, indicates that a well-planned and well-taught local area study can enhance children's mapwork skills. It also suggests that some upper juniors are able to recognise the extent and limitations of their local area knowledge and to represent this on maps.

Research background

Research into children's map understanding and mapmaking (Boardman, 1983; Matthews, 1992; Wiegand, 1993) involves a variety of approaches (Catling, 1996). Important links have been established between children's mapmaking and their environmental experience, spatial understanding and learning of adult conventions in map representation (Matthews, 1992).

As mapmakers, children appear to use a number of understandings and competencies by the time they are aged about ten or eleven. These include:

- using their experience and knowledge of a locality to identify and select features and pathways
- drawing maps of the locality with recognisable spatial accuracy
- depicting features and areas in detail on their local area maps
- increasing use of 'plan view' style to represent features
- drawing on experience of maps to present information in conventional forms
- recognising that what they include on their map does not show every detail in an area

However, within any given age group there will also be a range of achievement in mapmaking, local knowledge, spatial awareness and the use of map conventions (Matthews, 1992).

Methodology

A study was devised by the author to explore the impact of teaching about maps and the local area on children's ability to draw maps of their locality. The project was undertaken in a south-west London school with 34 nine- and ten-year olds from a year 5 class: 16 boys and 18 girls. Past research has indicated gender differences in environmental knowledge and mapping competence (Matthews, 1992) so evidence of this was under scrutiny. Before and after their study, the children were asked to draw from memory a freehand map of their own locality. The maps were analysed for the range of the locality knowledge shown and for the way in which cartographic conventions were used. The children were interviewed about their experience in using the local area.

The project lasted for most of one term. It involved a variety of activities designed to increase the children's knowledge of the local area, to develop their geographical understanding and to enhance their map skills. These included:

- study of land use in the locality (an urban area about a kilometre square)
- undertaking an urban trail designed to cover a variety of land and building use in the locality
- gathering data on shop types, evidence of change, traffic density, shoppers' habits and adults' ideas about the extent of the neighbourhood
- study of recent and earlier editions of large-scale OS maps and of photographs to find out about parts of the area not visited
- use of local street maps to identify routes around the area
- making maps to represent information and understanding about the area
- study of information on the area from the local authority's planning department

Results

The maps drawn before and after the local area was studied showed the variety of local area knowledge and map competence among the class. Comparisons of Figures 1a and 2a and Figures 1b and 2b show the variation between individual children.

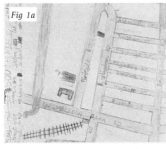

Fig 1a

Fig 2a

Fig 3a

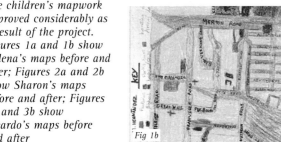

Fig 1b

Fig 2b

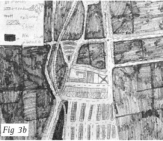

Fig 3b

The children's mapwork improved considerably as a result of the project. Figures 1a and 1b show Helena's maps before and after; Figures 2a and 2b show Sharon's maps before and after; Figures 3a and 3b show Ricardo's maps before and after

Range of locality knowledge

It was clear from the maps and from interviews that there was a wide disparity in experience and knowledge of the area among the children. All the children had been resident locally for more than two years (32% since birth) and had considerable experience of using the central shopping area. The distribution of homes was skewed to the east of the area (to the right of the railway line in Figures 1b and 3b). All were used to walking to the shops, though 74% of the children used a car if the family were in a hurry or the weather wet or cold.

There was a clear link between the home range of the children and the maps drawn before the start of the project, supporting other research evidence (Matthews, 1992). These maps also showed that most children had some sense of the spatial layout of the area (Figure 1a), though this was not always accurate (Figure 3a). Boys had more extensive knowledge than girls of the area but were not more accurate spatially.

The maps drawn after the study indicated that learning about the local area had an impact on children's understanding of the extent of the area and its spatial layout. This is evident in Figures 1b, 2b and 3b. It is noticeable that while in one case the area drawn is larger (1b), in the other (3b) the child recognises that he is not knowledgeable enough to depict the 'not sure about it' areas. Figures 1b and 3b are typical of 77% of the group, while Figure 2b indicates the weakest representation of local knowledge.

All the post-study maps showed that the children had a more extensive and informed knowledge of the area than before. This is not to say that they were necessarily all accurate; Figure 2b contains many errors. Nor are 1b and 3b perfect. However, there is evidence to indicate that a detailed study of a locality with clear objectives will improve children's knowledge of the area. The results also showed that the difference in local area knowledge between boys and girls still existed after the project but was less significant than at the start.

Use of map skills

The pre-study maps showed that while the majority of children were able to draw an area using plan view (e.g. Figure 3a), some 9% of the children drew pictorial maps (e.g. Figure 2a) and 38% used a mix of plan and pictorial representation. All the initial maps focused on features and in the main provided information about buildings and roads. Some 32% of the children included a key (Figure 1a). Children were able to map the area and in some cases drew on previous learning about how to show features on a map.

The post-study maps demonstrated that all the children had learnt about the conventions of maps, and 18% had developed (at least in the short term) an understanding about using a map to represent their knowledge of the area rather than just information about it. They also showed that children had begun explicitly to represent areas on maps.

All children developed a sense of map representation. Figure 2b indicates that the child has made the basic move from showing places of personal interest in pictorial form to the use of 'regular' (ruled) lines, colour and names to show information on a map. Figure 1b draws heavily on conventions developed by the class for representing information about land use; it uses colour symbols especially, but a church symbol is also deployed. This was common. Figure 3b is also 'conventionally' informative about key features and building use in the central area; however, the map is also used to show the extent of this child's confidence about his knowledge of the area. Figure 3b shows 'what I know' and 'what I don't know'. In both pre- and post-study mapping there was no difference between the girls' and boys' mapping skills.

There is useful evidence to show that teaching about the way maps represent environments can help children develop their understanding of the 'conventions' which maps use, such as keys and a range of symbols suited to a purpose. Where the focus shifts to the careful and accurate mapping of places, some children seem able to grasp the idea that maps can show what they know and need not simply be 'filled in' in order to look complete.

Conclusions

There are two conclusions to be drawn from this research. One is that study of a local area, if well-prepared and thoroughly taught, is likely to improve children's knowledge of the area and develop their awareness of its spatial layout. This will vary from child to child. It is probable that those with a more detailed and extensive knowledge at the start of a local study will make as much or more progress than those with less accurate understanding. The second is that the planned teaching of map skills will improve their use. In making their own maps children will not necessarily draw on OS map conventions but most will use a 'conventional' style. If children are enabled and encouraged through their local study to recognise the extent and limitations of their knowledge of the area, some may begin to represent this on their maps.

The implications for teaching are important. It is vital to plan a range of active experiences so that local area studies can develop children's *knowledge* of local features, *understanding* of geographical ideas and the use of appropriate *skills* such as fieldwork and mapwork. In addition, *values* and *attitudes* should be explicitly developed. These include encouraging children to be confident enough to represent their ignorance and uncertainty, as well as their confidence, on their own maps.

References

Boardman, D. (1983) *Graphicacy and Geography Teaching.* London: Croom Helm.

Catling, S. (1996) 'Technical interest in curriculum development: a programme of map skills' in Williams, M. (ed) *Understanding Geographical and Environmental Education: The Role of Research.* London: Cassell.

Matthews, H. (1992) *Making Sense of Place.* Hemel Hempstead: Harvester Wheatsheaf.

Wiegand, P. (1993) *Children and Primary Geography.* Lewes: Falmer Press.

Children's Understanding of Nested Hierarchies

Doug Harwood

An important objective of primary geography is to teach young children that places exist in a nested relationship, in which smaller places are located inside larger places, e.g. house within street, district, town, county, country and continent. Research suggests that this central idea is often misunderstood, even by older primary pupils, although there is some evidence that learning can be accelerated by systematic teaching and enriched experiences. Children's comprehension of nested hierarchies should therefore be assessed on a regular basis. Possible methods and research findings are discussed below.

Verbal tests without cues

In this approach, children are asked to respond to structured questions without any help from verbal, physical or pictorial cues. Piaget and Weil (1951) asked Swiss children about their homeland and nationality, using questions such as: *Where do you live? What is Switzerland? Where is Geneva? Are you Swiss?* Children up to nine years old mainly saw Switzerland as another place existing alongside Geneva. Later, Switzerland was recognised as a place surrounding rather than including Geneva. Only at eleven years old was the nested relationship understood (p. 565).

Jahoda (1963) interviewed 144 Glaswegian children between six and eleven, asking: *Where is Glasgow? Where is Scotland? What is Scotland? What is Britain? Have you heard of Britain? What do you think it is?* Jahoda categorised children's replies into four stages (Figure 1).

Jahoda found that 86% of six- and seven-year olds had no conception of Scotland as part of Britain (Stage 3). Even at age ten and eleven, 35% could still not express the Glasgow-Scotland-Britain relationship correctly (Stage 4). On average, children from middle class areas performed better than those from working class areas, suggesting that environmental factors may be important.

Stage 1	No conception of Glasgow as a unitary whole
Stage 2	Conception of Glasgow as a unitary whole, but had no conception of it as part of Scotland
Stage 3	Conception of Glasgow as part of Scotland but no conception of Scotland as part of Britain
Stage 4	Glasgow - Scotland - Britain relationship correctly expressed

Figure 1. Jahoda's four stages of place understanding

Daggs (1986) used a verbal test without cues with American children aged six to nine years. He included questions such as: *Are the people in (town X) in Pennsylvania? Can a person leave the USA and remain in Pennsylvania? Would you explain that to me?* The results showed that many found the tests difficult.

Harwood and McShane (1996) replicated Jahoda's verbal test with children aged five to ten living in the Nuneaton area and found that, although many still experienced difficulties, general levels of understanding appeared to have improved since Jahoda's study. They suggest that increased media exposure to place knowledge, greater opportunities for travel and enriched learning programmes encouraged by the National Curriculum may account for the improvement. They conclude that introductory work on nested hierarchies at key stage 1 is justified.

The use of Jahoda-type, structured verbal assessments has been criticised for the following reasons:
- the language is too controlled and limited by the researcher's frame of reference;
- the young pupil may not understand the questions, especially those involving place names, in the same terms as the researcher;
- the children might provide correct answers which do not fit the researcher's categories (e.g. Q. *Where is Stratford?* A. *Near to Warwick*).

The use of follow-up verbal tests with cues (e.g. multiple choice questions) may overcome this problem. Verbal assessments should always be supplemented by exercises using models, pictures and maps of the locations in question.

Pictures and models of familiar situations

Children first become acquainted with the idea of nested locations in the home (e.g. the toy is situated in the drawer, in the cupboard, in the bedroom, in the house). Teachers of infants might begin by helping children to describe the toy's address in the home or classroom, with the aid of models and pictures.

Daggs (1986) introduced a model of a park and used vocabulary which was more familiar to the children than that used in a conventional verbal test. The children were asked questions, e.g. *If you were in the sandpit, could you be in the playground? Would you explain that to me?* Their understanding was much greater than was the case with verbal tests without cues, with even the youngest achieving almost total success (p. 697). This shows that hierarchical place relationships can be understood when presented in a familiar form and context.

Mapping activities

Some researchers have asked children to draw their own maps of nested relationships. Piché (1981) used such methods during Piagetian-type interviews with children in London aged five to eight years. She discovered that they had many misconceptions about the relationship between their home, London and England. Although the six-year olds knew their address, they did not know what it meant (p. 52). The children had 'no spontaneous construction of extended places' and a 'poor concept of neighbourhood'. They seemed to 'remember places in terms of their own actions, independent of a geographical framework' (p. 66). Only 5 out of 48 children understood that they could live simultaneously in both London and England (p. 75).

When Harwood and McShane (1996) asked their pupils to assemble a jigsaw map of the British Isles and locate England, Nuneaton and their home on the map, they found that the children understood nested relationships better than they did in the Jahoda-type interview (p. 21). Similarly, Harwood and Fotheringham (forth-coming) asked children aged 10-11 years to draw their own map of Stratford, Warwickshire, England, Britain and Europe following a Jahoda-type interview (Figure 2). They found that, on average, the pupils performed one level higher in the map-drawing exercise than in the interview. They also discovered that Jahoda's assumption, that children's understanding of nested hier-archies progresses concentrically, i.e. from home town to country, was not borne out by the evidence. In the interviews, the children were more likely to locate Stratford in England than in Warwickshire and, interestingly, England in Europe than in Britain. They concluded that the more steps there are in the spatial hierarchy, the more likely that concentricity will break down.

Symbolic representations

In order to test how far children's verbal abilities had influenced the results, Jahoda (1963) devised a spatial test using geometric shapes to symbolise Britain, Scotland, England and Glasgow: a rectangular black card = Britain; two smaller rectangular pieces of white card = Scotland (smaller) and England (larger); a small brass disc = Glasgow. The children were asked to arrange these shapes in the correct spatial relationship (p. 54). The results showed that 87% of six- and seven-year olds and 60% of eight- and nine-year olds were still at the lowest level. Performances in the spatial test were much inferior to the verbal test. Nearly 75% of the children, who had been able to state correctly that Glasgow is in Scotland, did not demonstrate this understanding in the spatial test (p. 55). Daggs (1986) used a similar test, in which a circle was drawn to represent Pennsylvania. The children were asked to draw another circle to represent a town in Pennsylvania and to colour Pennsylvania. Many of the six- to nine-year olds had problems with this test.

All the research, albeit based upon small samples, indicates that many primary children have difficulty in understanding the nested relationship of places, unless the tasks are presented in a concrete form, within a familiar context. However, evidence from Harwood and McShane (1996) suggests that learning can be accelerated by systematic teaching, involving stimulating resources and experiences. Teachers should therefore exploit every opportunity, whenever places are being discussed across the

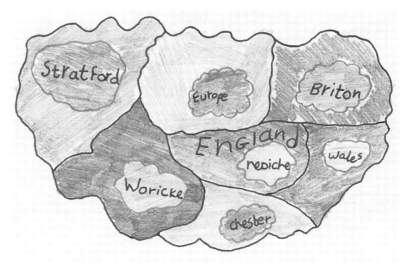

Figure 2. Map showing the relationship between Stratford, Warwickshire, England, Britain and Europe, drawn by a child aged ten

curriculum, to reinforce the idea of nested hierarchies. Monitoring such progress requires regular assessment, involving a combination of methods. Research suggests that some forms of assessment may be more difficult than others (Figure 3).

Most difficult

↑
- Arranging and/or drawing symbolic representations
- Verbal tests without cues
- Pupils drawing their own maps
- Pupils shading and marking maps already drawn
- Verbal tests with cues, e.g. multiple choice questions
- Discussing models or pictures of familiar locations
↓

Least difficult

Figure 3. Assessment techniques arranged in order of difficulty

Teachers might start with the assessment method which they think is most likely to challenge the pupils and then gradually simplify or complicate the process until the child's level of competency is identified.

References and further reading

Daggs, D. (1986) as cited in Downs, R., Liben, L. and Daggs, D. (1988) 'On education and geographers: the role of cognitive developmental theory in geographic education', *Annals of the Association of American Geographers*, 78, 4, pp. 680-700.

Harwood, D. and McShane, J. (1996) 'Young children's understanding of nested hierarchies of place relationship', *International Research in Geographical and Environmental Education*, 5, 1, pp. 3-29.

Jahoda, G. (1963) 'The development of children's ideas about country and nationality', *British Journal of Educational Psychology*, 33, pp. 47-60.

Piaget, J. and Weil, A. (1951) 'The development in children of the idea of homeland and of relations with other countries', *Institute of Social Science Bulletin*, 3, pp. 561-578.

Piché, D. (1981) 'The spontaneous geography of the urban child' in Herbert, D. and Johnston, R. *Geography and the Urban Environment: Progress in Research and Applications*, IV. Chichester: John Wiley, pp. 229-256.

Progression and Gender Differences in Mapwork

Sarah Taylor

Mapwork and spatial awareness are fundamental to geography. However, there is still no general agreement about the way children develop mapwork skills. Furthermore, there is considerable speculation about differences in the abilities of boys and girls.

Research background

Wiegand (1993) suggests that geographical skills surface at a very early age. Children often attempt to draw maps or pictures of places before they can read or write. These skills need to be exploited so that they may be developed to their full potential at a later stage.

Norris Nicholson (1993) believes that maps are what drive children to become curious about the wider world. She also argues that maps and plans are integral to many people's lives. There has been a great deal of research into gender differences. Matthews (1984) found that girls tend to represent people and landmarks whereas boys tend to show paths, cars and other forms of transport. Boardman (1990) argues that 'as they grow older, boys consistently perform better than girls, of the same age, in map-drawing tasks'.

It has been widely observed that boys are given more opportunities to explore their surroundings without supervision than girls. Hillman (1993) also notes that, owing to social and cultural factors, English children are much more restricted nowadays than they were in the past. This is likely to have an effect on spatial awareness.

There is no agreed hierarchy of mapwork skills, and researchers have suggested different ways of assessing children's progress and achievements, (see Figure 1).

A research project

This involved 263 children aged between four and eleven in a large urban primary school. 122 boys and 141 girls took part in the study. Most of the children came from middle-class homes.

In order to assess their mapping ability the children were all asked to imagine the following situation:

> You are organising a party and people are coming to your house from all over town. To make sure that everyone gets to your house on time, you decide to draw a map to send out with the invitations. Try to cover as wide an area as possible, and do not forget to include any features which may help your guests to find their way.

Before they began the task, the children looked at examples of Ordnance Survey and other printed maps. They were then split into single-sex groups and given a sheet of A4 paper and fifteen minutes to complete the work. No help was given during the drawing time. Questions about the use of colour, keys, symbols and so forth were answered with the statement 'If you believe it will improve your map'.

Results

The maps were given a numerical grade from 1 to 5 for each of the criteria shown in Figure 2. The scores were then aggregated to give a rating for overall mapping ability. The results showed that boys tended to cover a greater area and were more likely to use plan views than girls (Figures 3 and 4). The boys also produced a wider range of map types. However, the girls drew more details and were more accurate than the boys beyond the age of eight. They were also more inclined to be co-operative and worked harder at the task they had been given.

It would be interesting to carry out a comparative study in a different geographical and socio-economic area. It would also be valuable to concentrate on Special Educational Needs as some of the children in the group showed exceptional abilities. The Geography National Curriculum programme of study contains specific references to mapwork skills, as do the Level Descriptions. Further research is needed to find out what can and should be achieved by primary schoolchildren.

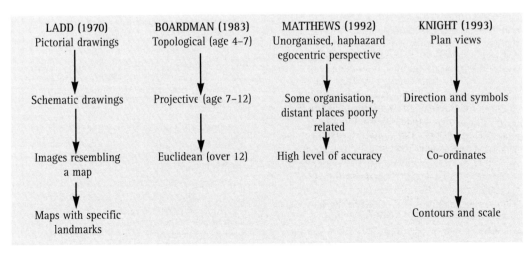

LADD (1970)	BOARDMAN (1983)	MATTHEWS (1992)	KNIGHT (1993)
Pictorial drawings	Topological (age 4–7)	Unorganised, haphazard egocentric perspective	Plan views
↓	↓	↓	↓
Schematic drawings	Projective (age 7–12)	Some organisation, distant places poorly related	Direction and symbols
↓	↓	↓	↓
Images resembling a map	Euclidean (over 12)	High level of accuracy	Co-ordinates
↓			↓
Maps with specific landmarks			Contours and scale

Figure 1. Different approaches to progression in mapwork

Area covered	The boys' maps generally covered a larger area than the girls'. Single children and those with younger siblings portrayed greater distances than those with older brothers and sisters.
Features shown	In all age groups girls showed a greater awareness of shops and services. Street furniture and traffic appeared frequently in maps drawn by both sexes.
Accuracy	The accuracy of the maps increased steadily with age. The boys were consistently more accurate below age eight, but the girls were more accurate after that.
Scale	The ability to draw to scale increased with age. Boys and girls performed similarly.
Organisation	The maps ranged from those showing discrete features and very little spatial organisation, to highly organised and well-thought-out representations. There was no significant difference between boys and girls.
Plan view	In every age group the boys' maps were more sophisticated.
Labels	Children under the age of six failed to use any labels. Over this age the use of labels increased steadily, especially road names.
Keys, grids and symbols	Colour was used more prominently by the girls. Only nine children (eight of them boys) added a grid.

Figure 2. Summary of results

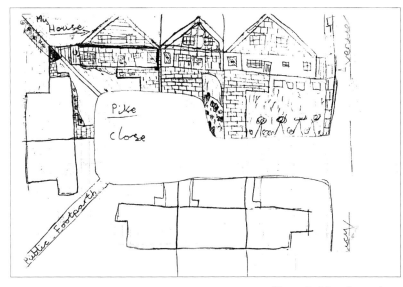

Figure 3. Map drawn by girl aged eleven

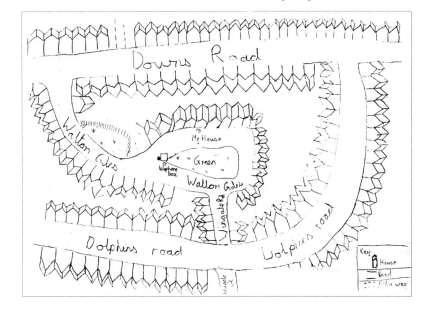

Figure 4. Map drawn by boy aged eleven

References

Boardman, D. (1983) *Graphicacy and Geography Teaching*. London: Croom Helm.

Boardman, D. (1990) 'Graphicacy revisited: mapping abilities and gender differences', *Geography Educational Review*, 42,1.

Hillman, N. (1993) *Children, Transport and the Quality of Life*. Policy Studies Institute.

Knight, P. (1992) *Primary Geography Primary History*. London: Fulton.

Ladd, F. C. (1970) 'Black youths view their environment; neighbourhood maps', *Environment and Behaviour, 2*, pp. 74–9.

Matthews, M. (1984) 'Environmental cognition of young children', *Transactions of the Institute of British Geographers* 9, pp. 89–105.

Matthews, M. (1992) *Making Sense of Place*. Hemel Hempstead: Harvester Wheatsheaf. (1993).

Norris Nicholson, H. (1993) *Inspirations for Geography*. Scholastic.

Wiegand, P. (1993) Children and Primary Geography. London: Cassell.

Aerial Photographs and Understanding Places

Christopher Spencer

Some theorists have argued that aerial photographs require so much cognitive interpretation they can only be used with children from mid-primary school age upwards. However, the weight of research evidence suggests that infants and pre-school children can interpret them successfully, especially if they show a familiar area at a reasonably large scale.

Film makers often open with an 'establishing shot' before they get into the action of the film, so that the viewer knows how to locate all the subsequent action. It might be a long view of the street, or a distant view of the house in which the characters live; or, interestingly, the shot may be an aerial view of the key location. Geographers often do the same when they assemble photo-packs as classroom resources. The first picture shows an aerial view of the whole area – maybe an island. Subsequent pictures provide details about the daily lives of the people who live there.

And now the National Curriculum suggests children should use aerial photographs at key stage 1. Does this seem unremarkable? Sensible? We all know from classroom experience that young children enjoy working with aerial photographs but their capacity for this kind of work has been fiercely contested. In particular, Liben and Downs (1992), two American researchers, have raised all manner of doubts. The argument has an impact beyond the research

journals. Those who question children's ability to handle aerial photograph are actively delaying map and aerial work in the American equivalent of the National Curriculum until the mid-primary years.

The doubters are reinforced in their views by Piaget's theories which claim that young children should indeed be cognitively incapable of handling aerial perspectives. You will remember that at this age they are still deemed to be egocentric, and they obligingly fail Piaget's 'three mountains' experiment.

The Three Mountains Experiment

Can young children appreciate that their view of the world may not be the same as that of someone who is viewing it from a different position? Piaget thought not, and devised a task to test his view. In the experiment, papier mâché models of three separate mountains were placed on a table top with a toy to represent the 'other person'. The child sat at the table and stayed in the same position while the experimenter moved the toy person around the model. The child was asked what the toy person would 'see' from each position. Egocentric children always reported that the toy saw what they saw; non-egocentric children described views that they thought the toy person might see.

As with all tests of this kind, the responses given may be highly dependent on the nature of the instructions. Indeed, more recent research has shown that with subtle changes to the methodology or instructions, even pre-school children can appreciate the possibility of alternative perspectives.

Researchers have now accumulated a body of evidence to show that children of young primary age can work with aerial views and the simpler forms of maps (Blaut, 1997a). Even children as young as four years old (and maybe even younger) can give perfectly intelligent answers

Figure 1. Children as young as four can scan oblique aerial photographs and deduce features

Photo: PhotoAir

when asked to identify objects represented in aerial photographs of an unfamiliar area (Sowden *et al.*, 1996).

Research background

One of the first studies was conducted by Jim Blaut who, together with David Stea, pioneered research at Clark University in Worcester, Massachusetts on very early geographic education. Puerto Rican and American pre-schoolers (four-year olds) recognised whole categories of geographical items when they were shown vertical aerial photographs. When Merrie Muir (see Blaut, 1997b) was teaching map skills to first graders (six-year-olds) she found that she needed something substantive in order to illustrate her ideas. Together with Roger Hart she experimented with a number of different approaches. One of these involved making three-foot square ozalid (or blueprint) copies of nine inch by nine inch vertical aerial prints and joining them together on the classroom floor as a composite image. Not surprisingly the children were fascinated by this representation of their local area. They walked and crawled over it, tracing routes and journeys. They also used it for fantasy games and more formal work such as locational exercises involving toy cars, ambulances and locomotives. In a further experiment a group of nine-year olds (third graders) were taken up in a small plane above Chicago in order to explore their understanding still further. The excitement and involvement this generated was immense, but for most of us the flying classroom is not a practical proposition!

During the 1990s experiments have been carried out in many countries. Pre-school children have been asked to work with photographs of different scales and viewpoints (vertical and oblique) and to identify specific features on black and white and on colour prints. Tests have also been devised to see if children are able to 'drive' a toy car along specific routes. The results from places as diverse as Mexico City, Chicago, Sheffield, Tehran, Taichung and Durban all indicate that young children are able to interpret aerial perspectives. Even more significantly, they can do this whether or not they have access to TV, films and other media.

These pre-school children seldom had problems with scale, as Piaget and his followers claimed they would, nor were they content simply to describe the geometry of an image (e.g. a wiggly line), but tried instead to give specific features their proper names (Figure 1).

Classroom implications

Most of the early studies made use of small-scale black and white vertical images of areas that were unfamiliar to the children. When young children are given large-scale colour photographs of an area that they know well they identify more kinds of features and more features in total. Interestingly they also explore the image in ways which immediately suggest teaching points and issues for discussion. It may take children time to recognise that a photograph shows their own area but once they make the connection their enthusiasm is immense. They trace routes eagerly, remark upon how much nearer some

things are to others they had not known about, and discover hidden areas. For example, teachers have reported observations from children such as *I didn't know they had a swimming pool* when studying an aerial view of a prosperous housing area.

Oblique aerial views are easier for children to interpret than vertical views. Spencer *et al.* (1997) conducted a detailed investigation with over 80 nursery school children in two different Sheffield schools. They found that while children could identify some elements, such as houses and cars, equally easily on both types of photograph, they had great difficulty with some other features. For example none of the children could identify a fence during free responses (i.e. spontaneously), only 14% could interpret it when it was pointed out on the vertical image, but 63% were able to recognise it on the oblique view.

Summary

Given what is now known from research, it is clear that young children can readily understand and work with aerial images and that these images are conceptually within their grasp. Thus, it would certainly seem appropriate to use aerial photographs as 'establishing shots' from which teachers can develop discussions about the character of the local area. They can also use aerial images to investigate questions such as *Who lives there? How do people travel from place to place? Where do they go for enjoyment and relaxation?* With older children, more detailed studies can be undertaken, for example using overlays to show what they would value and protect in the area shown, and what and how they would change it.

References and further reading

Blades, M., Blaut, J., Darvizeh, Z., Elguea, S., Sowden, S., Spencer, C., Stea, D. and Uttal, D. (1998 in press) 'A cross-cultural study in young children's mapping ability', *Transactions of the Institute of British Geographers*.

Blaut, J. (1997a) 'Children can', *Annals of the Association of American Geographers*, 87, pp. 152-158.

Blaut, J. (1997b) 'Piagetian pessimism and the mapping abilities of young children', *Annals of the Association of American Geographers*, 87, pp. 168-177.

Liben, L. and Downs, R. (1992) 'Developing an understanding of graphic representation in children and adults; the case of GEO-graphics', *Cognitive Development*, 7, pp. 331-349.

Sowden, S., Stea, D., Blades, M., Spencer, C. and Blaut, J. (1996) 'Mapping ability of 4-year old children in York, England', *Journal of Geography*, 95, pp. 107-111.

Spencer, C., Blades, M., Hetherington, D., Sowden, S. and Craddock, S. (1997) 'Can young children use aerial photographs as cues for navigation?', *Proceedings of the Royal Institute of Navigation*. Oxford Conference, Oxford, RIN.

Stea, D., Blaut, J. and Stephens, J. (1996) 'Mapping as a cultural universal' in Portugali, J. (ed) *The Construction of Cognitive Maps*. New York: Kluwer Academic Publishers.

Learning from Photographs

Margaret Mackintosh

The assumption is often made that photographs are easy to understand, and we take it for granted that children and adults see the same things in a picture. But research and experience suggest that this is not so. The skill of looking at pictures needs to be taught.

Brief summary of previous research

Previous (rather dated) research into how children see geographical pictures has mostly focused on how nine- to sixteen-year old pupils interpret physical landscape features. There is one study, however, which involved seven-year olds (Long, 1953), and this has provided some valuable observations:

- Seven-year olds seem not to see a picture as a whole but as a series of apparently separate details selected at random.

- Young children tend to notice the foreground and large background objects and ignore the middle ground. They do not 'see' the whole picture.

- Detail is important to many seven-year olds.

Subsequent research has confirmed that the need for detail decreases with age (Bayliss and Renwick, 1966).

These findings were recently re-examined by two students, Katherine Stott and Nicola Eaglesham, as part of their BEd degree course. It was expected that as children were exposed to more pictorial images (TV, video) they would be more competent in interpreting photographs.

Research methodology

Both students used coloured photographs although Warwick (1987) claims there is no evidence that colour plays a role in what children see. Working in East Kent, Stott (1994) showed children in Reception and years 2, 4 and 6 four photographs for ten seconds or less. In an interview they were asked to recall what they had seen, and then helped to interrogate the pictures with questions including: *What can you tell me about where this picture was taken?* and *How do you know?*

Eaglesham (1997) adopted a different approach. She asked children to label black and white photocopies of different pictures (with reference to a coloured photograph), make drawings and answer questions. These tasks were designed to explore observation, perception and interpretation (especially preconceived ideas). Questions included the familiar: *Where is this place? How could we get there? How is it similar to other places you know? What do you feel about this place? Would you like to visit it?*

Most of the pictures were selected from photo-packs of 'less developed localities' (Brace, 1992;

Bunce *et al.*, 1992). The subjects included an urban street in St Lucia, rural water collection in Kenya (Kapsokwony) and an oblique aerial view of a Welsh village from the key stage 1 geography SATs (1993). The SATs material was used first since if children cannot obtain information from a photograph of an environment familiar to them (i.e. a UK scene) they could hardly be expected to use photographs of unfamiliar environments (Bayliss and Renwick, 1966). All the pictures used had clear fore-, middle- and background detail.

Eaglesham also analysed the picture content of ten well-known educational photo-packs. She found they were predominantly about daily life, but tended to include too many static, posed images or people-less landscapes that failed to stimulate discussion (Figure 1).

Findings

Summarising from four photographs - an office interior, a bus station, Dover docks, and Guildford High Street - Stott found that:

Reception children focus first on big things, things they know, recognise and can name, then size and colour become important

Year 2 children pick on lots of detail, especially foreground detail, including things that are relatively unimportant to the understanding of the photograph including peripheral objects, but not necessarily the main essence of the picture (e.g. in the office picture they noticed the phone but not the people)

Year 4 children concentrate on the main essence and associated objects, but detail is less important than getting a basic understanding of the picture

Year 6 children get a grasp of the picture and generalise.

Eaglesham found that the number of items year 2 children labelled was related to neither size (both large items and minute detail being noted) nor position. However, their drawings featured foreground and background items, whereas middleground items tended to be ignored (Figure 2). She also found that children's responses were influenced by preconceived ideas, evidenced by the inclusion of items not actually present.

Conclusions

Visual literacy has been compared with print literacy in that both employ a similar process: identifying, decoding and interpreting symbols. In addition, prediction, observation, supposition and narrative are also needed to understand both print and images.

Visual perception is a form of information processing which changes with age. The findings confirm previous research, and suggest that children do not see the photograph as a whole, but look upon it as a series of different parts which they favour according to individual preferences, interests, familiarity and language. Their interpretation, evidenced by questioning,

Theme	Occurrences
Daily life	36
Farming	34
School and health	32
Landscape	25
People posed	22
Transport	21
Retailing	20
Homes	16
Crafts and clothes	13

Figure 1. Contents of pictures in ten geography photo-packs (seven rural, three urban)

Photo: Vincent Bunce

Figure 2. Elspeth's drawing of a St Lucia street scene only shows foreground and background details

appears to be influenced by past experience, geographical language, emotional content, imagination, stereotypes and preconceived ideas.

Classroom implications

From the literature and this research some conclusions for classroom practice can be drawn:

- Children need to be taught to read and interpret photographs, through planned directed study with progression. This should start with simple ground level pictures at KS1 and progress through increasingly complex pictures to oblique and vertical aerial photographs, since different perspectives of people and places require separate means of interpretation. (Wiegand, 1992)

- Care should be exercised in selecting published photo-packs. Rural images can reinforce stereotypes of material deprivation - mud huts, bare-footed natives and arid dusty landscapes - and confirm the notion that the western way of life is superior, ignoring the great cities and architectural wonders of Africa, South America and southern Asia (Graham and Lynn, 1989).

- Teachers should select pictures that challenge, rather than confirm, children's existing frameworks, exploiting their curiosity and flexible attitudes about other peoples and cultures. Choosing positive images can help to correct stereotypes and negative media bias.

- Asking them to give a picture a title helps children to take in the whole image and to generalise. It is also helpful to direct their attention to fore-, middle- and background.

- Check that the children see what is intended. Give them a line drawing or field sketch of a picture and ask them to shade/colour/annotate certain features. Alternatively devise 'land-use' activities from a photograph, possibly using tracing.

- Encourage children to take on the role of photographer. This will help them appreciate that photographs have limitations and may present biased and/or stereotypical images. It will also help them to develop an analytical approach and realise that photographs do not tell the whole truth.

- Use structured questions to develop children's interpretation skills. Chambers (1996) suggests a sequence of increasing complexity: concrete, descriptive, speculative, reasoning, evaluative and problem solving.

- Develop visual literacy alongside print literacy - both important life skills.

References

Bayliss, D. G. and Renwick, T. M. (1966) 'Photograph study in a junior school', *Geography*, 233.

Brace, S. (1992) *Kapsokwony: Rural Kenya*. Action Aid.

Bunce, V., Foley, J., Morgan, W. and Scoble, S (1992) *Focus on Castries, St Lucia*. Sheffield: Geographical Association.

Eaglesham, N. (1997) 'How do infant children interpret photographic representations of distant environments?'. Unpublished dissertation. Rolle School of Education, University of Plymouth.

Graham, J. and Lynn, S. (1989) 'Mud huts and flint: children's images of the third world', *Education*, June, pp. 29-32.

Long, M. (1953) 'Children's reactions to geographical pictures', *Geography*, 180.

NCC (1993) *Geography KS1 SATs*. NCC.

Stott, K. (1994) *Teaching Geography Using Photographs*. Unpublished dissertation. Canterbury Christ Church College.

Warwick, P. (1987) 'How do children see geographical pictures?', *Teaching Geography*, 12, 3.

Wiegand, P. (1992) *Places in the Primary School*. London: Cassell.

Geographical Vocabulary

Hugh Ward

Primary school children are sometimes confused about geographical terms. Teaching strategies, especially involving practical experience and visual illustration, are needed to help children think about geography and language, interpret situations and grasp the meaning of particular words.

The Geography Order for KS1 and KS2 refers rather tersely to the need for pupils to use geographical vocabulary to describe their surroundings (paragraph 3a of the programmes of study). However there is little guidance on what terms children should use, or how their acquisition of language will be enhanced by geographical words.

One way of gaining a wider perspective is to analyse the overall language requirements of the programmes of study. This reveals that at KS1 the bulk of the vocabulary is to do with directional terms and naming human features. By contrast, at KS2 more attention is given to processes and physical features. These findings are in line with a similar study of the 1991 Order by Scoffham and Jewson (1993-4). This identified 130 words which either appeared in the programmes of study or were implied by the statements. Two fifths of these terms were to do with human features and activities and one tenth with environmental quality.

Specialist vocabulary

Vocabulary research is usually conducted on the basis of the frequency with which a word is used. This approach was followed by Milburn (1974) who compiled a list of terms used in geography textbooks and classroom work. Milburn asked the children to define these words using verbal answers, writing, drawings or diagrams. The proportion of correct definitions only rose from 9% in year 3 to 30% in year 6 and many basic terms were still imperfectly understood in the early secondary school years (Figure 1).

alp	equator	north pole
antarctic	erosion	ocean
bar	estuary	plain
basin	fog	river
canal	gorge	snow
cape	irrigation	swamp
chain	lake	tributary
cliff	marsh	valley
confluence	mountain	wind
continent	mouth	

Figure 1. Problem words for year 6 children (after Milburn)

Naming places

Hart's wide-ranging research into children's experience of place in a suburban township in the eastern United States (1979) was a rare attempt to link geography with psychology.

Hart took the child in his or her phenomenal landscape as the unit of study. His findings stress the significance of language in developing children's experience. Names enable children to differentiate the landscape into a multitude of places. Although children share a common language with adults, Hart notes how children also invent personal names and distinctions. Writers such as AA Milne and Mark Twain use this child culture immortally in their stories but it has been neglected in educational research.

Further insights into the child's personal lexicon comes from Jones (1989) who analysed essays about everyday experiences written by primary school boys and girls living in a Manchester suburb. The children described play activities after school in the garden, on the local recreation ground, golf links, woods and derelict spaces. Their responses not only revealed the environments which the children valued but also showed how intense were their feelings about it.

Language and thought

Vocabulary and concept development are complementary aspects of intellectual development. However, while children may use verbal labels attached to concepts, tasks involving classification often reveal they have little understanding of the concept itself (Gagne, 1997; Milburn, 1974; Vygotsky, 1962).

The importance of informal, spontaneous learning of words for young children's conceptual development has long been known. Vygotsky (1962) showed how everyday language provides a foundation and structure for learning more abstract and systematic concepts. He suggests that everyday vocabulary and 'scientific' terms mutually reinforce each other. Teaching that relies on definitions and parrot-like repetition alone accomplishes nothing but empty verbalism. Milburn (1974) too notes that increasing verbal fluency does not always lead to conceptual understanding.

It cannot be assumed then that children will understand simple terms such as 'beach', 'hill' and 'river'. Homonyms (words which have a variety of meanings) and homophonic words (words which sound the same but have different spellings) present particular problems. However a number of researchers (Gagne, 1997; Milburn, 1974; Devlin, 1994) have found that practical work leads to a marked increase both in the vocabulary that children use and the precision with which they apply it. First hand experience and fieldwork have a crucial role to play.

Gagne's research and writings demonstrate conclusively that learning subject vocabulary is a prerequisite for higher forms of learning. The most elementary tasks involve verbal associations and verbal sequences. The ability to discriminate is fundamental if children from the earliest age are to distinguish parts of their environment and build classifications. Early learning at school places heavy emphasis on perceptual differentiation and naming objects, spaces and events.

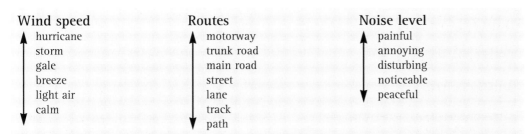

Wind speed	Routes	Noise level
▲ hurricane storm gale breeze light air ▼ calm	▲ motorway trunk road main road street lane track path	▲ painful annoying disturbing noticeable ▼ peaceful

Figure 2. Some environmental word scales

In the past, it was assumed that a word acquired its meaning by occurring *together* with the thing which it meant or stood for. Current thinking still emphasises the importance of experience to the process of language learning but places greater weight on the general context, immediacy and purpose of things and events. Modern research has also been concerned with helping children think *about* language (Donaldson, 1978, 1992). Bearing in mind these findings, it is difficult to envisage a stronger case for enmeshing geography language acquisition with practical activity and real-world experience.

Enhancing learning

Much vocabulary learning concerns understanding concrete features with naturally defined boundaries 'playground', 'shop', 'volcano' for example. Some terms, however, are more abstract and not visually perceptible. Working with a small group of six-year olds Miller (1997) found that the children had a very limited understanding of basic 'compass' vocabulary. Further enquiry involving photographs and word cards revealed problems with terms such as 'valley', possibly because it is harder to visualise a gap than the surrounding hills and mountains.

Miller also identifies several 'associate word groups' in which the children considered that different terms had the same meaning. Examples include wood/forest, coast/shore, mountain/cliff and river/stream/lake. This problem is related to an important strand in geographical thinking concerning sequences that lack self-evident or visually perceptible boundaries. The Beaufort Scale, for example, identifies separate categories for wind conditions such as 'calm', 'light air' and 'breeze'. In reality these all form part of a continuous scale. Work on scales and sequences can help to develop children's understanding. If, as juniors, they learn some of the common conventions for describing slopes, weather and other geographical features, this will help them to make sense of higher-order concepts such as relief and weather systems in later years (Figure 2).

The way forward

Geographical terms first become part of a child's 'mental dictionary' through first-hand exploration in pre-school years. As they grow older children expand their vocabulary adding experiences both inside and out of the classroom. Depending on the environment - urban, rural, coastal, upland - children's encounters with their surroundings will vary greatly. Equally their home circumstances are likely to contribute to their understanding in an unsystematic way.

The development of children's geographical vocabulary and the role of language in learning geography is potentially a rich field for enquiry. The words we use express our ideas and influence what we observe and think. The relationship between language and ideas is unquestionably a central intellectual problem. Is language a tool by means of which we *create* our world?

References

Devlin, M. (1994) 'Geographical vocabulary in the junior school' *Issues in Education* (*The Canterbury Papers*), Canterbury Christ Church College, 2, 1 pp. 26-30.

Donaldson, M. (1978) *Children's Minds*. London: Fontana.

Donaldson, M. (1992) *Human Minds*. Harmondsworth: Penguin.

Gagne, R. (1997) *The Conditions of Learning*. London: Holt, Rinehart and Winston.

Hart, R. (1979) *Children's Experience of Place*. New York: Irvington.

Jones, A. (1989) 'The feeling tone of childhood' in Slater, F. (ed) *Language and Learning in the Teaching of Geography*. London: Routledge, pp. 141-148.

Milburn, D. (1974) 'Children's vocabulary' in Graves, N. (ed) *New Movements in the Study and Teaching of Geography*. London: Temple Smith, pp. 107-120.

Miller, T. (1997) *Directional and Landscape Vocabulary*. Unpublished student study. Canterbury Christ Church College.

Scoffham, S. and Jewson, T. (1993-4) 'Geographical language (1 and 2)' and 'A glossary of terms (1 and 2)' *Primary Geographer*, 13-16.

Vygotsky, L. (1962) *Thought and Language*. Cambridge Mass.: MIT Press.

Ward, H. (1991) 'Children's language and geography' in *Primary Geography Matters - Inequalities*. Sheffield: Geographical Association, pp. 47-49.

Using the School Grounds

Debbie Bartlett

Agenda 21 encourages young people to undertake practical activities to improve their surroundings, and to make links between local and global issues. Where better to begin than the school grounds? What follows here is a description of some specific projects and initiatives that have been tried with infant and junior classes.

Primary school teachers have used the school grounds as an outdoor classroom for teaching curricular and extra-curricular subjects for some time. The potential is enormous. It is estimated that the 24 000 primary schools in England have

---

THE VISIONING BRIEF

- Think about what YOU VALUE in your surroundings.

- What are the school grounds like now? You could do a survey using the plan provided as a base to trace from (if it needs up-dating please let us know). Perhaps you could talk to people and see if you can find out why the grounds are as they are. Do you have any particular problems? How can these be addressed? Who is interested? What do they think?

- What sort of place would you like your grounds to be? Everyone can be involved in the visioning process pupils, staff, dinner ladies, visitors, local people and don't forget the wildlife you share your site with; they were probably there first!

- Discuss the answers to these questions and

- FORMULATE YOUR VISION

Present your ideas fun, fantasy and functional on an A1 plan and in an A4 file (up to 50 pages) in any form you like.

PERHAPS WE CAN HELP YOU TOWARDS ACHIEVING IT

Figure 1. This visioning brief was given to teachers on the entry form for the project. The brief was meant to be a prompt rather than a blue-print for work with children

combined grounds of 60 000 to 70 000 hectares (DES, 1990). However, while many school grounds have been developed to support a wide range of educational activities, there is evidence that the potential is not realised and that school grounds are a wasted resource (Titman, 1994). 1996 saw the publication of two relevant reference works. One of these, *Teaching Environmental Matters Through the National Curriculum* (SCAA,1996), deals particularly with the geography and science curriculum but stresses that the environment and environmental issues can feature in almost any subject. The second, *Our World - Our Responsibility* (RSPB and CEE, 1996), discusses the formulation and implementation of a 'whole-school environmental education policy' and the cross-curricular approach. It relates closely to Agenda 21 and the concept of sustainability, both of

which feature increasingly on the primary school agenda.

Many of the professionals who work on school grounds feel that school communities should be more involved in the design and management of their own grounds to meet their own needs for delivering the National Curriculum, for extra curricular activities and for fun. Every school is different in its culture, and in the constraints and opportunities offered by the physical nature of its surroundings. While all schools are increasingly under pressure of time and money there is still enormous interest in making the most effective use of the resource offered by the school's immediate environment.

There are clear links between the geography curriculum, environmental education and the development and on-going management of school grounds. Projects which explore these issues are also directly in line with Agenda 21 (see pages 34-35) which encourages young people to undertake practical activities to improve their surroundings. Kent Property Services (KPS) Landscape Department have been applying visioning techniques to school grounds to encourage children to articulate their ideas.

Visioning is a process that has become popular over the last decade, particularly in the USA, as a means of building a consensus between groups that hold very different, but equally valid perceptions of the community environment they live in. Visioning is an approach which fosters participation and brings different strands and interests together hence its value in schools, where adults and children work together in a common, shared environment.

School grounds visioning project

The school grounds visioning project which was run in conjunction with Canterbury City Council was originally developed in response to the problem of litter in school grounds. Visioning techniques were used to find out what schools felt was important about their environment and to promote the concept of looking after the things they valued. This was seen as the first step towards encouraging children to care for the environment as a whole in their visions for the future (Figure 1).

Vision 21 for schools

A schools' competition (Vision 21) was launched on National School Grounds Day 1995, with all schools in the Canterbury district invited to take part. Teachers were supported by an after-school question session, and given large copies of site plans and an entry form outlining what was required. All the schools were visited after their visions had been submitted, to give children and teachers an opportunity to talk about their work and discuss the way forward.

The visions appeared in many different forms, with plans and surveys, analyses of opinion polls, and inspiring and imaginative options for the future presented in a range of media. Differences in form and content reflected the nature of the sites, the character of each school community and the problems which concerned them. But some issues were important to almost every school. These included the problem of mud and litter, the lack of things to do in the playground, the need for recycling facilities and, inevitably, the shortage of money.

In addition to giving advice and support to individual projects, the Council provided all schools with litter bins and helped them to set up recycling schemes. KPS Landscape Department ran workshops for teachers on making paving slabs, tree dressing and sundials and gave out free copies of the *Trees from Seed* manual.

Other projects

Other local authorities in partnership with KPS are now involved in similar initiatives which take a holistic approach to school grounds and involve the whole school community. For example, Gillingham 2000 for Schools was launched on School Grounds Day 1996; Swale Vision 21 for Schools was set up in September 1996; and Quality Environment for Dartford (QED) began in 1997. The basic methodology has been kept the same but local help and sponsorship has increased and the time scale extended to a full year so that as much as possible can be done within the curriculum.

Agenda 21

Agenda 21 emphasises that young people have an important role to play *now* and as responsible adults of the *future* (see pages 34-35). A balanced programme of environmental education can help them to make informed choices and alert them to the environmental consequences of their decisions (Figure 3). Responses to the various projects revealed that there were many active groups (including the children's parents) engaged in taking care of the school environment. To emphasise the links between school grounds and Agenda 21 all participating schools are given a copy of *Rescue Mission Planet Earth - A Children's Guide to Agenda 21* (United Nations, 1994). This has now become an integral part of the project and is handed out with the site plans and entry forms.

Workshops for teachers are another development. These are run by KPS and the Wider World Development Education Project and introduce Agenda 21 and the basic concept of sustainability. Participants are also shown how the school grounds can be used as a model to engage all the members of a school in decision making. The roles of the school grounds are considered - aesthetic, recreational, as an educational resource and as a habitat for humans and wildlife - and the impact of changes made in the grounds is estimated. The final session makes links to other countries and cultures, bringing aspects of geography to life and reinforcing the slogan used in the first visioning project:

**WE NEED TO SAVE THE PLANET
THINK GLOBALLY - ACT
LOCALLY
BEGIN THE PROCESS IN YOUR
SCHOOL GROUNDS**

GILLINGHAM 2000 FOR SCHOOLS

Teachers at one infant school began by asking the children what they felt about the school grounds and were surprised with their unanimous desire to have something done about the library mobile. This was something of a shock as it was a new feature of which the school was justly proud. Specifically the children wanted the gap beneath it filled in, the door without a handle removed, curtains instead of bar blinds, the colour brightened up and a 'proper roof ' put on.

The gap under the mobile was quickly filled in and the door without a handle obscured with a poster. Dinosaurs are a theme of current projects and an artist has helped the children to paint them on the outside of the building.

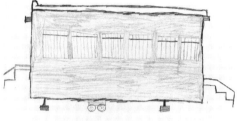

Figure 2. Asking children for their views can produce some surprising results

Figure 3. Many schools develop a stewardship concept with the children producing posters for display around the grounds

References

DES (1990) 'The outdoor classroom. Educational use, landscape design and management of school grounds', *Building Bulletin 71*. DES.

RSPB and CEE (1996) *Our World - Our Responsibility. Environmental Education: A Practical Guide*. RSPB and CEE.

SCAA (1996) *Teaching Environmental Matters Through the National Curriculum* . London: SCAA. Titman, W. (1994) *Special Places; Special People. The Hidden Curriculum of the School Grounds*. WWF.

United Nations (1994) *Rescue Mission Planet Earth - A Children's Guide to Agenda 21*. London: Kingfisher.

Defining Localities

Rachel Bowles

It has been observed that understanding of the character of a locality changes with the age of the user of that locality; it is also known that gender and freedom to roam affect the depth of knowledge about a locality. But what other factors affect the definition of locality from a child's point of view?

Research background

The earliest studies of children's understanding of their immediate environment began in the 1950s and by the 1970s several studies of children's behaviour in the physical environment had been made with a view to improving the teaching of fundamental geographic concepts at primary level. Hart (1979) and Matthews (1992) give full summaries and references while Blyth and Krause (1995) make suggestions for furthering similar investigations in a modern, urbanised world. Spencer, Blades and Morsley (1989) and Spencer and Blades (1993) have shown how a child's spatial awareness and competence increase with maturity. Environmental range is a term often used to denote locality knowledge, and different influences are recognised - gender, parental concern, social constraints and the character of the urban landscape (Cullingford, 1992) - all play their part. Much, then, has been studied and much is now known, but still the question of how far a child's immediate locality extends remains to be explored (Wiegand,1992).

Children's ideas about their locality

In a study of schools in London and elsewhere (Bowles,1995) children discussed their favourite places, completed questionnaires and used local maps to 'finger walk' journeys and mark destinations. Evidence from the studies showed that not only did a child's idea of locality expand with age but the size of the locality increased the further one moved from an urban centre (Figure 1). Observations about the 'core' locality - the area agreed upon by both KS1 and KS2 children - are summarised in Figure 2.

Ideas about the core locality

'Locality' as understood by children meant those places visited regularly and these did not always accord with the non-geography teachers' conception of the locality, because the school staff often lived away from the local area.

The core locality was identified as the same for all age groups and was usually determined by walking distance to school, the nearest post office and general stores.

The size of the core area was coincident with the concept of the whole locality if it also contained all the needs of the community for special as well as everyday requirements. This usually meant a choice of supermarket and stores, fresh food and other markets and a variety of entertainment.

Figure 2. Children's perceptions of their core locality

The study also showed that mobility, in the form of personal transport, affected the size of the local area travelled. Inner city areas cannot accommodate cars; rural areas rely upon cars and bicycles for reaching basic services. This could alter the natural perspective of a child's environmental range. The widest concept was found in outer suburbs and rural villages seeded with commuter families who used cars for work and reaching amenities.

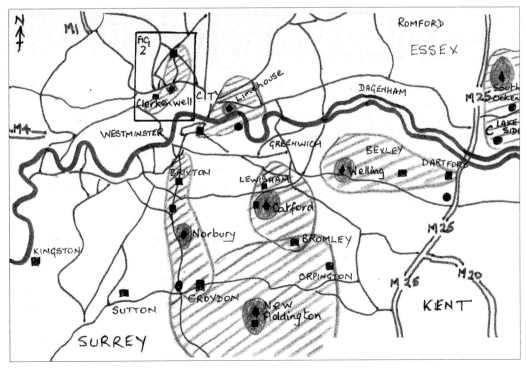

Figure 1. Children's ideas about the size of their locality varies considerably between inner London and suburban schools

How the notion of locality changes with age

In July 1997 the research was extended to a second set of schools in widely varied localities. Year 5 children completed a questionnaire either individually or as groups with their teacher to investigate the depth of their locality knowledge (Figure 3).

Survey questions

1. Think of your home locality - you have to take a visitor or friend round to show them where the main places of interest are in your area. Make a list of these places.

2. How would you answer the question *Where do you come from*? (This is the sort of question you get when away on holiday!).

3. What can you tell someone from another place about what makes your place important? What does it make? Has anyone written about it? Who visited it in the past? Now? Who was born there?

4. What other place is it most like?

5. What other place is very different from it?

Figure 3. Questions used to investigate children's ideas about their locality

In no class were all the children able to answer the question about their address (Question 2) - alarming by this age. Responses to Question 3 revealed how, unless the school had made conscious efforts to maintain observation in the locality in every previous year, the children's natural observations were eroded. This was particularly noticeable in socially disadvantaged localities. Questions 4 and 5 were inadequately answered by suburban children for they were the groups with the least sense of community and cohesion.

In discussion it was often the less able child who was most resourceful and observant about the landmarks and features of the locality even though they could not write their address correctly or give an accurate location. Conversely, the more academic child, who had been taken to many places outside the locality and knew the location of home and school, could not perceive the relationships between landmarks and features which they dismissed as unimportant. Clearly the school has a role to play in developing an ability to articulate awareness for the one group, and a sense of place for the other.

There were a number of other significant conclusions. First, children made full use of open spaces, parks, woods and playing fields if they were within walking or cycling distance. This has important implications for town planners. Second, when a school had used the local area for both historical and geographical work the children had developed an understanding of the importance of the locality by the time they reached year 5. Some children, usually boys, were aware of local work opportunities especially if connected with sport or cars. On the whole, however, economic activity was an unknown quantity which evoked little curiosity. It had no place in the children's lives even though their living conditions were influenced by the presence or absence of work.

Implications

It would seem that children are more likely to come to an understanding of their locality if their teacher knows and walks the same places as they do. Further, the teacher who recognises the constraints presented by both community and family and devises outdoor activities in the locality can only widen horizons for the children. The locality is much more than the current community and this should be recognised and investigated.

Teaching about the locality need not and should not be repetitious; different topics can be tailored to each year's needs but should, in the end, add up to a well defined picture of our place. As Figure 4 shows, there is a recognisable sequence in a child's understanding of his/her locality. Schemes of work could be geared to this, ensuring a progression from one year to the next, and providing opportunities to focus their learning by telling an audience about their new knowledge.

1. Absolute certainty about the core of the area known to them. This shows itself as a willingness to describe features without prompting, debate another person's view of those features and begin to enquire into the reason for the features human or physical. This is the area visited most frequently.

2. Acknowledgement of a fringe area within which they have secure knowledge of certain features but keep each discrete, e.g. the toyshop in town, the boat by the river.

3. The KS2 child will give a fuller picture of the extent of this larger area, define its limits and can be prompted to raise questions about its character. This provides the framework for increasing geographical perceptions of a defined locality.

Figure 4. Stages in the growth of a child's idea of locality

References

Blyth, A. and Krause, J. (1995) 'Children's spatial awareness: an enquiry' *Primary Geographer,* 20, pp. 26-27.

Bowles, R. (1995) 'How well do you know your locality' *Primary Geographer,* 23, pp. 16-18.

Cullingford, C. (1992) *Children and Society.* London: Cassell.

Hart, R. (1979) *Children's Experience of Place.* New York: Irvington.

Matthews, M. H. (1992) *Making Sense of Place.* Hemel Hempstead: Harvester Wheatsheaf.

Spencer, C., Blades, M. and Morsley, K. (1989) *The Child in the Physical Environment.* Chichester: John Wiley.

Spencer, C. and Blades, M. (1993) 'Children's understanding of places: the world at hand' *Geography,* 78, 4, pp. 367-373.

Wiegand, P. (1992) *Places in the Primary School: Knowledge and Understanding of Paces at Key Stages 1 and 2.* Lewes: Falmer Press.

Places, Attachment and Identity

Stephen Scoffham

Children have a natural desire to explore their surroundings. Through play and other transactions they come to make sense of their place in the world and invest their environment with meaning. Not only are these experiences vital components of a child's emotional and psychological development, they are also important educationally. Geographical enquiries, investigations and fieldwork have a key role to play in promoting environmental knowing.

From the moment they are born children start learning about their surroundings. Their first perceptions are of the home environment. Starting with their parents and immediate family they begin to find out more about the place where they live. Gradually the range and detail of their perception increases. By the time they go to school most children are aware of the world around them and have acquired a definite notion of their own identity. They are, in short, young geographers and they carry with them a wealth of ideas and experience.

Figure 1. Forces influencing eight-year olds as they explore the environment (after Hart)

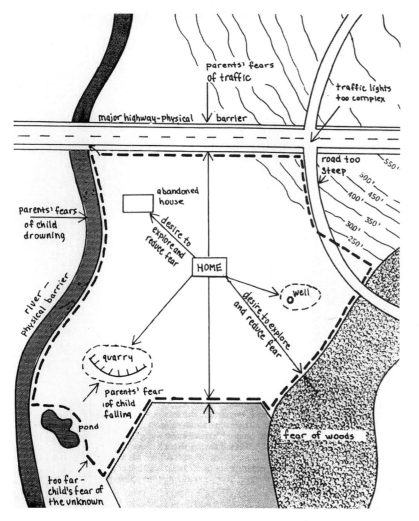

The way in which children learn about places is complex and researchers are only slowly piecing together the story. Part of the problem is that there is no entirely logical or inevitable sequence of events. Learning is for many people a surprisingly idiosyncratic process in which ideas are acquired in an apparently random manner. Most people do not become systematic thinkers until they reach adolescence, or even later.

It is also remarkably difficult to discover what is actually going on inside a child's head. We were all young once but it is impossible to recapture the sense of awe and wonder which children experience on doing something for the first time. Adults can often only observe and deduce what seems to be happening from the outside. As one commentator put it:

> Our present-day knowledge of the child's mind is comparable to the fifteenth century map of the world - a vast mixture of truth and error ... vast areas remain to be explored.

Exploring the local environment

Most of us remember the place where we were brought up in some considerable detail and often recall it with fondness. These first impressions of the outside world stay with us throughout our lives and provide a rich source of experience. Authors such as Laurie Lee, Virginia Woolf and Marcel Proust recall their early memories with great sensitivity in their novels. Our sense of identity, it seems, derives in some part from the social and physical environment in which we spend our childhood.

The way children interact with the immediate surroundings is important not only for their psychological well-being, it also promotes their educational development. Many play activities involve rehearsing or re-enacting previous events and situations. Through imitation children are able to give full reign to invention and fantasy. Piaget argues that make-believe play allows children to assimilate knowledge and forms the basis of a child's thought even before it can speak. Certainly the opportunity to model and manipulate experiences seems to be an essential part of the learning process.

Private geographies

Several researchers have attempted to find out more about children's private geographies. One of the key studies was undertaken by Hart (1979) who made a detailed study of a New England township over a two year period. Hart discovered that the children put a particularly high value on water features such as rivers, lakes and ponds. They also favoured woods and trees for climbing and hiding games. The places they feared matched the archetypal scary places of children's literature - attics, cellars and abandoned buildings and bedrooms and garages at night. Very few of the children selected places for their aesthetic qualities alone.

Hart comments on the way children treasure informal routes and pathways which they often use as 'short-cuts' even when they are actually longer. Other researchers, too, remark on children's affinity for secret routes and alleyways. As they explore their surroundings children construct private geographies which meet their physical and emotional needs (Figure 1).

Naming places

Further insight into children's thinking is provided by the names children invent for their favourite places. Matthews (1992) reports how, when drawing maps of suburban Coventry, children labelled a variety of local features. Examples included the 'Moth-hawk tree', the 'Dump', 'Charlie's field' and the 'Back Alley'. Sometimes these personal names denote the activities that are associated with a place rather than its appearance, e.g. 'Roller-coaster place'.

It is worth remembering in this context that the most intensively used play areas are often small patches of dirt. Children need places where they simply loiter or day dream. Edmund Gosse, the Victorian naturalist, is one of many authors who has left us with a description of his childhood pleasures:

> By the side of the road, between the school and my home, there was large horse pond ... Here I created a maritime empire islands, a seaboard with harbours, lighthouses, fortifications. My geographical inventiveness had its full swing. Sometimes, while I was creating, a cart would be driven roughly into the pond, shattering my ports with what was worse than a typhoon. But I immediately set to work, as soon as the cart was gone and the mud had settled, to tidy up my coast-line again and scoop out anew my harbours.
> *Gosse, 1965. p. 136*

The quest for meaning

It is through transactions of this kind that children come to invest their environment with meaning. The attachment to places which we develop as adults is derived from these childhood interactions. We identify with our home area in lots of different ways. Some people support their local football team, others become involved with local history or trace their family tree. Historically people used to believe they belonged to the soil of a particular place in an organic and religious relationship. The Romans recognised the spirit or essence of a locality (its *genius loci*) by setting up shrines to local deities. Anthropologists have recorded similar beliefs among the original inhabitants of Australia and North and South America.

These studies remind us that the quality of an environment is a very complex issue. What a place is like is not simply a matter of fact. It equally depends on how we perceive it and what we feel about it.

Today, concerns over personal security and the relentless growth of road traffic are serving to erode children's personal freedom and their links with the environment. In an authoritative study Hillman (1993) found that the number of unaccompanied activities undertaken by junior school children at weekends had halved between 1971 and 1990 (see also pages 28-29 in this book). He comments on the way this may affect their emotional and social development. When children explore the environment they have opportunities to take initiatives, learn survival skills, develop a sense of adventure, gain self-esteem and accept responsibility for their actions. The physical activity also helps to keep them fit and healthy.

The importance of fieldwork

Restoring this richness to children's lives is a challenge which schools cannot expect to meet on their own. However, they can at least promote children's awareness and provide some form of environmental experience. Geography fieldwork has a unique contribution to make to this process. On one level fieldwork can consist of environmental walks and simple data collection activities in and around the school building. It can also involve work in local streets and journeys to nearby places. In addition many schools organise some form of residential experience or school journeys.

Investigating the quality and character of different places is an essential component of any worthwhile geography curriculum. Children are uniquely equipped to undertake these studies as they have a freshness of vision and a strong natural desire to explore their surroundings. As the nineteenth century philosopher Freidrich Froebel put it: children 'seek adventure high and low' in their 'desire to control the diversity of things' and 'see individual things in their connection with a whole' (Lilley, 1967). We need to encourage them in this endeavour from the earliest age.

References

Gosse, E. (1965) *Father and Son*. London: Heinemann.

Hart, R. (1979) *Children's Experience of Place*. New York: Irvington.

Hillman, M. (1993) *Children, Transport and the Quality of Life*. London: Policy Studies Institute.

Lilley, I. (1967) *Friedrich Froebel: A Selection from his Writings*. London: Cambridge University Press.

Matthews, M. (1992) *Making Sense of Place*. Hemel Hempstead: Harvester Wheatsheaf.

This article is abbreviated from Scoffham, S. 'Children as Geographers' in Carter, R. (ed) *Primary Geography Handbook* (in press). Sheffield: Geographical Association.

Neighbourhood Safety

Mayer Hillman

The local neighbourhood used to provide a unique place for children to develop basic physical, social and geographical skills without adult supervision. However, parental fears about the dangers of traffic and possible molestation by strangers has led to growing restrictions being placed on children's freedom to get around on their own. Public policy should be changed so that children are again free to explore their local area.

Governments have always viewed the home and the school as the proper *loci* for children's development. What is overlooked is the complementary role that the neighbourhood can play. Many of the key skills needed for the transition from the limited capabilities of childhood to the prospective independence of adulthood can be acquired there. It is a unique place for learning, *without adult supervision,* how to cope in the real world. It represents an informal classroom containing opportunities for children to give rein to instinctive desires to enlarge their geographical boundaries and to extend their physical and social capabilities.

Few sociologists, child psychologists or educationalists have recognised the value for children of gaining permission, almost invariably from parents, to get around on their own in this local environment. As a result there has been very little research in this area and the long-term consequences of reducing children's freedom have been largely unnoticed.

Travel patterns

In the early 1970s, we carried out surveys in schools in different parts of England, ranging from an inner London suburb to a rural parish in Oxfordshire (Hillman *et al.,* 1973; Hillman *et al.,* 1976). We asked the children to complete questionnaires about their patterns of travel and about their weekend leisure activity outside the home. We replicated these surveys in the same schools almost a generation later (Hillman *et al.,* 1991). The findings reveal a marked increase in restrictions imposed by parents on the autonomy of their children. More and more children are escorted on their school and leisure journeys – and at an ever-later age. For instance, we found in the earlier surveys that 80% of seven- and eight-year old children went to school on their own, while twenty years later, the proportion had declined to 9% (Figure 1).

A much lower proportion of children now walk to school and whilst most own a bicycle, few are allowed to use it as a means of transport in spite of the fact that, given safe routes, it is ideal for their independent mobility and also for

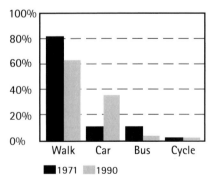

Figure 1. Method of travel to school by English junior school children, 1971 and 1990

promoting their health. The effect of this limitation is to restrict the size of their geographical catchment area since, in terms of travel time, the bicycle catchment is ten to fifteen times greater than the walking catchment.

Children's access to their local surroundings has been steadily diminished as parents seek to minimise their exposure to possible injury or molestation. And the surroundings themselves have changed, often in ways that diminish their value as 'activity areas' for children. For example, the appropriation of some streets exclusively for traffic and parking has meant children have lost what were effectively outdoor public spaces for them to use. Also, the quality of many urban neighbourhoods has declined as a result of traffic noise which interferes with children's outdoor activities, inhibiting comfortable communication. Traffic also pollutes the air with fumes which, as well as causing or exacerbating various ailments, probably promotes shallow breathing, resulting in less well developed lungs.

One consequence of these restrictions and losses is that the children affected are far less likely to be able to learn how to make decisions *when on their own*, how to act responsibly and how to assess the motives of those they do not know. They are less likely to be able to have adventures, extend personal frontiers, be mischievous, learn directly the consequences of being careless, gain self-esteem and self-confidence from acting sensibly, and contribute to family and community life by shopping, visiting or running errands for old people. These are all essential components of growing up and developing geographical understanding.

Parental attitudes

Our surveys involved enquiring into parents' attitudes (Figure 2) and it emerged that their greatest concern is the growing risk to children from motor vehicles. These perceptions are by no means groundless; transport statistics on the volume of traffic show that, in the last twenty years, the number of cars on the roads has almost doubled. During the same period, over 130 000 child pedestrians and cyclists have been killed or seriously injured, mainly through no fault of their own – unless normal carelessness in child behaviour is to be treated as blameworthy. One reason for the increased risk of road casualties is that the average speed at which vehicles travel is higher: on roads subject to a thirty mph limit, over two in three car drivers and one in two lorry drivers now break the law by exceeding the limit (Department of Transport, 1997). Another reason is that, due to design 'improvements' vehicles can accelerate to higher speeds in less time, thereby requiring pedestrians and cyclists to move quicker and to exercise greater vigilance.

Another area of parental concern revealed in our surveys relates to child assault and molestation on the streets. But this risk must be seen in perspective: children are far more likely to be murdered by a person known to them, and far more are killed by strangers in motor vehicles than by strangers on foot! One consequence of parents' fears is that more of children's waking hours are spent under the watchful eye of an adult. (A recent MORI poll has recorded three in ten respondents saying that, as a means of crime protection, they always use a car rather than go by public transport or on foot.)

Hidden consequences

Children's loss of independent mobility is not the only largely unnoticed consequence of growing dependence on the car. A growing body of research suggests that their declining fitness is attributable to the fact that they walk and cycle far less. National Travel Survey data covering the last twenty years show that annual mileages on foot and cycle among those of school age have declined by over 25% and 40% respectively. Increasingly sedentary lifestyles are both a cause and a consequence of greater confinement to the home. This does not bode well for children's future health: we may have a time bomb on our hands which will explode in twenty or thirty years when the incidence of heart disease rises sharply owing to lack of daily exercise during the critical years of childhood.

Other policy initiatives have led to reinforcing a view that children's independence outside the home is unimportant. For example, the wider exercise of parental choice regarding their children's school often results in selecting a school which is more distant from the home. This makes it less likely that children will walk or cycle to school, and more likely that they will be chauffeured by car – adding to traffic problems for people living along the route. There is a knock-on effect in that a child living near the school may lose a place to the 'incomer' and so have to travel further as a consequence, again generating more traffic. Given the urgent need to curb vehicle use and promote more sustainable methods of transport, this is clearly an undesirable outcome. Dependence on car travel also tends to result in limits on participation in extra curricular activities after school. Friendship patterns, too, may have to be more formally arranged because children are less able to drop in on each other in a casual way.

Even apparently laudable initiatives, such as the *Safe Routes to School* projects, reflect the conventional view that children's lives are largely school-oriented and that protecting children from various traffic hazards means making the school journey safer. This overlooks the fact that children make many more journeys in their free time to destinations other than school. So why not *Safe Routes for Children* instead?

New priorities

At the heart of the problem lies society's careless attitude to children – the assumption that formal education and protection from risk of injury are of such overriding importance that they justify taking away children's independence outside the home. In effect, society appears prepared to condone the practice of withdrawing children from danger rather than taking measures to bring about the withdrawal of danger from children. Some maintain that children today are better-off: they have far more access to people

and places. On the other hand, it could be argued that by overlooking the effects on their development, we are breeding a generation of 'battery-reared' children – qualitatively very different from earlier generations of 'free-range' children, with all the generalised implications such an analogy has both for their freedom and for their health in its widest sense.

The educational effects are equally disturbing. It is through free transactions with their environment that children learn to follow routes, develop a sense of direction and build up their sense of personal identity. A knowledge and understanding of their own environment is also vital when it comes to making comparisons with other places in more distant parts of their future world. These are key elements of a meaningful geographical education and this is reflected in the current Geography National Curriculum which requires children to learn about specific places at each key stage.

With evidence of the deleterious effects of growing restrictions on the independence of children outside the home, it is difficult to believe that a civilised society will not wish to reverse the process which has brought that about. We need to rethink policy. It should embrace the full spectrum of children's lives so that they are able to spend more of their leisure time in the outdoor environment *on their own* – as we or our parents did at their age – rather than being so heavily focused on the home and on formal education in school, important though these are.

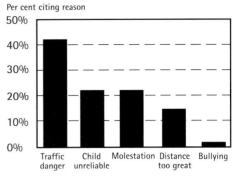

Figure 2. Reasons given by English parents for restricting junior school children from coming home alone from school

References and further reading

Department of Transport (1996) *Transport Statistics Great Britain.* London: HMSO.

Hillman, M. (ed) (1993) *Children, Transport and the Quality of Life.* London: Policy Studies Institute.

Hillman, M. with Henderson, I. and Whalley, A. (1973) *Personal Mobility and Transport Policy.* Political and Economic Planning.

Hillman, M., Henderson, I. and Whalley, A. (1976) *Transport Realities and Planning Policy.* Political and Economic Planning.

Hillman, M., Adams, J. and Whitelegg, J. (1991) *One False Move: A Study of Children's Independent Mobility.* London: Policy Studies Institute.

Moore, R. (1990) *Childhood's Domain: Play and Place in Child Development.* Moore Berkely, California: MIG Communications.

Ward, C. (1977) *The Child in the City.* London: Architectural Press.

Children's Ideas about the Environment

Bill Chambers

Children's perceptions of the local environment, their knowledge and attitudes to environmental issues and their ideas about the conservation of animals, have been the subject of various studies. Among other things, they demonstrate the value of using a range of techniques and adopting a multicultural perspective.

The local environment

A study conducted by a student teacher (McCloud, 1995) used drawings and interviews to study children's perceptions of their environment. The school in which the study was undertaken is in an inner city area dominated by massive gasometers and surrounded by terraced housing.

The children were given a list of eighteen adjectives - five positive and thirteen negative - to describe the local environment. The words which they chose most frequently were 'lovely' and 'beautiful' (reception), 'dirty' (years 2 and 4) and 'ugly' (year 6). As their age increased, so did the number of different negative words.

The children were then asked to draw their preferred environment. Many of the children in the reception class made imaginative drawings showing, for example, the gasometers with queens living in them. The year 2 children tended to select beautiful features such as the sun, trees, flowers, water, beach and sand. By year 4 the children were beginning to include more active components of the environment such as swings and slides. In year 6 football pitches and swings and slides comprised 70% of all features drawn. The most commonly drawn feature for all pupils in the school was the sun. It is possible that these choices may be linked to the lack of play space and sunlight associated with the school and surrounding terraced housing.

Table 1. The words children used most frequently to describe their ideal environment

Reception	nice	lovely		
Class 2	nice	beautiful		
Class 4	exciting	beautiful	lovely	
Class 6	exciting	interesting	beautiful	lovely

Making a better place

In another study (1996) the Liverpool 8 Children's Research Group surveyed 575 children in ten inner city primary schools. The children were asked the following question by local people trained in interview techniques: *If we wanted to make a better place for children to live in, what would you like us to do?* They were invited to choose from a range of 38 solutions derived from the ideas of a representative 'focus group' of children. The top six preferences in rank order were:

stop selling and taking drugs
stop strangers picking up children
stop guns and knives being sold and used
give homeless people somewhere to live
take care of animals
stop people being robbed

This shows the children's dissatisfaction with a violent and criminal environment and a concern to safeguard disadvantaged people and animals.

Elephants and conservation

Taking a completely different approach, Macheng (1995) studied the attitudes and knowledge of children in Botswana and Britain to the conservation of elephants. Five hundred children were involved in the study, including 24 year 6 pupils in a Merseyside primary school. The results of the study in the latter school are described here and compared with results derived from 250 secondary-aged Botswanans.

Knowledge of elephants

All the Merseyside children had seen an elephant in real life, over a quarter of them before starting primary school. The most common sightings and sources of knowledge are listed in Table 2.

Sighting	% children
zoo	71
circus	21
UK safari park	8
Knowledge	
television and videos	58
printed sources	17
zoos	17
cinema	8

Table 2. Elephant sightings and sources of knowledge

Characteristics of elephants

Children were asked to choose from a list of five adjectives describing elephants. Almost two thirds of the Merseyside group thought that elephants were *intelligent* and a quarter thought that they were either *very friendly* or *pretty and clean*. This contrasts with Botswanan pupils who thought elephants were *very destructive* (60%) or *dangerous* (34%). In another question, 29% of the British pupils thought that elephants *could kill humans* while this view was held by 100% of Botswanans.

Elephant conservation

Attitudes to elephant conservation differed markedly between the two groups: 96% of the Merseyside group thought that *elephants should not be killed under any circumstances* whereas in Botswana the figure was 1%. Similarly, 80% of the Merseyside children thought excess elephant populations should be *moved to other countries* while 64% of Botswanans favoured *culling*.

To the statement '*elephants should be killed for ivory*', 63% of the Botswanan pupils agreed but none of the Merseyside pupils. When asked about attitudes to the illegal killing of elephants for ivory the Botswanans were evenly split between *allowing the trade in ivory* and *giving poachers long prison sentences.* The Merseyside pupils were in favour of *a ban on the ivory trade* (87%).

Major environmental issues

Qualter and Leeson have published many questionnaire-based papers concerned with major environmental issues such as global warming, acid rain, rainforests, marine pollution, motor vehicles and asthma. Early papers were concerned with knowledge but more recently they have examined attitudes, values and management.

The greenhouse effect

Qualter *et al.* (1995) questioned 563 pupils between the ages of eight and eleven on the greenhouse effect. They were presented with twelve statements about ways to reduce the greenhouse effect and asked to tick one of five labelled boxes ranging from *I am sure this is right* to *I am sure this is wrong*. Scientifically acceptable statements were interspersed amongst other, less acceptable notions. The results indicate that the children were confused over possible solutions to the greenhouse effect (Table 3).

Qualter *et al.* concluded that these erroneous views are 'a combination of a misconception (that global warming endangers rare species) and a confusion between cause (global warming) and effect (the disappearance of rare species)'. They also contended that 'children have a generalised view ... so that anything which is said to be environmentally damaging might be considered to contribute to all environmental problems'.

Cars and the environment

Leeson *et al.* (1997) studied what a group of year 6 children thought about the consequences of increased numbers of cars and their ideas for reducing their environmental impact. Using procedures similar to those described above for Qualter *et al.* (1995), 165 children were asked to consider degrees of 'rightness' or 'wrongness' of different statements.

Three quarters of the pupils had a correct understanding about the possible consequences of increased numbers of cars on the greenhouse effect, smog, acid rain and asthma. However, they also held erroneous ideas about the effects on the ozone layer (75%), endangered species (59%) and rainforest destruction (50%).

When considering ways to reduce the environmental impact of car emissions, more than 75% correctly noted the use of battery-powered vehicles and economy of petrol use. Half realised that well maintained engines pollute less. The use of catalytic converters, streamlined cars and diesel engines were less well recognised as solutions.

This study suggests that children conflate ideas and generalise about pollution. Leeson *et al.* highlight a significant problem.

Conclusions

With regard to perceptions of the local environment and its problems, it seems that:
- children benefit from contrasting experiences

Correct	%
using recycled paper	83
avoiding car use	80
planting more trees	80
Erroneous	**%**
using unleaded petrol	92
reducing nuclear bombs	84
protecting rare species	85

Table 3. Solutions to the greenhouse effect

- schools and their grounds can provide peaceful natural and activity havens
- citizenship is an essential complement to environmental and geographical education
- the local environment needs support from the school and other local agencies.

When considering pollution we need to:
- provide factually correct information to children at an early age otherwise relearning will be needed later
- avoid using the word pollution as a general explanation for all environmental ills. Different forms of pollution (or pollutions) cause different effects.

The work on elephants highlighted how responses vary between peoples, cultures and places. We may wish to consider how to:
- present factually correct information and to offset the tendency among children to romanticise wildlife
- be critical of images and resources

presented by the media, commercial organisations and conservation agencies
- see issues from a non-British cultural point of view (i.e. avoid ethnocentricity)

Finally, there are methodological considerations. The differences between the McCloud and Liverpool 8 studies in terms of children's responses highlight the fact that the type of questions asked, the questioner and the social context of the question will all influence the children's responses.

References and further reading

Boyes, E., Chambers, W. and Stanisstreet, M. (1995) Trainee primary teachers ideas about the ozone layer, *Environmental Education Research*, 1, 2, pp. 133-145.

Leeson, E., Stanisstreet, M. and Boyes, E. (1997) Primary children's ideas about cars and the environment, *Education 3-13*, 25, 2, pp. 25-9.

Liverpool 8 Children's Research Group (1996) *Children's Needs Survey.* Unpublished.

Macheng, M. E. (1995) *A Comparison of Children's Knowledge and Attitudes to Elephants in Botswana and Britain.* Unpublished MEd. Dissertation, Liverpool Hope University College.

McCloud, K. (1995) *The Change in Children's Perception of the Local Environment from Reception to Year Six.* Unpublished Environmental Studies BEd Dissertation, Liverpool Hope University College.

Qualter, A., Francis, C., Boyes, E. and Stanisstreet, M. (1995) The greenhouse effect: what do primary children think?, *Education 3 to 13*, 23, 2, pp. 28-31.

Environmental Cognition in Young Children

Joy Palmer

Before they start formal schooling, most children have gained considerable knowledge about the world around them. However these ideas are often incomplete, blurred or even false, as is illustrated here with reference to a study of four-year old children's knowledge of two 'distant' environments. It also shows how important it is be aware of children's misconceptions when planning lessons on environmental issues and distant places.

The research involved interviews with 257 four-year old children living in North East England and California. Each child was shown photographs and interviewed individually by a trained researcher. The pictures were placed face down and turned over one at a time to prevent the children moving on before the discussion was complete. The children were also given plenty of time to think and respond. Interviews were tape-recorded and transcribed and the children's responses were grouped into categories to enable the extent of their knowledge and understanding to be assessed.

Cold places

A picture of snow-clad mountains and a glacier was recognised by almost all the children and 89% knew it would feel cold. Sixteen per cent were able to suggest where such a snowy place might be, the most common reply being *the North Pole*. When asked about forms of life which live at the poles, a third of the children gave correct answers, a third gave incorrect answers and the rest were confused. Figure 1 shows the different creatures the children thought lived in polar areas.

The children were asked what would happen to the snow and ice if the cold place became warm or even hot. Ninety per cent knew that changes of some kind would take place. Once again the

responses were categorised. Over half the children (61%) used the term 'melt', but it was clear they did not always have an adult understanding of the word. The idea that snow or ice just disappears or goes away was mentioned by 30% of the children. For example, they said *it just disappears* or *it would go away up into the sky*. One common misconception, shared by 16% of the group, was that the snow actually turns into grass or ground (soil).

When questioned about how creatures would be affected by the melting and disappearance of snow and ice, the most common response (21%) was that they would go and live somewhere else. A significant number of children (18%) thought that the animals would be able to stay even if the environment became hot. One child described an inverse hibernation theory: *they would go to sleep, 'cos they don't like warm places.*

Rainforests

When shown pictures of tropical rainforests and asked what they could see, 95% of the children made a valid observation such as *lots of trees* and 50% were able to give a possible name such as *rainforest, jungle, forest or wood*. About a third of the children were able to give at least one accurate fact about the climate or atmosphere: 18% regarded forests as dangerous or frightening places.

A consistent pattern of errors in the responses suggests that about a quarter of the children confused temperate and tropical forests, for they spoke of squirrels, mice and rabbits, and said it would feel cold and dry. Fourteen per cent referred to monsters, including dinosaurs. Only 2% could name a place where a tropical rainforest might be found. Very few children possessed accurate knowledge about the people of the rainforest. Any discussion of human life usually included reference to stereotypical ideas such as *people swing in the trees like monkeys.*

When asked why the trees might be cut down, almost 75% could think of a reason (not always accurate). Nearly a quarter (22%) thought it was something to do with the trees themselves, such as they were *too long* or *too old,* while 39% said it was because of people's needs, such as for making a fire, building a house or clearing space to make a road. One child even said *to get richer.*

Almost all the children could imagine how the felling of trees might affect forest creatures but very few expressed a causal link, such as *the animals will die or go away because they have no homes.*

Rubbish and recycling

Almost all the children (95%) could identify litter or trash in photographs and explain that it should be put in a bin or garbage can. Their knowledge of what happens after that was more limited, yet surprisingly extensive for children so young. Three quarters of the UK children mentioned 'bin men' and a third seemed to have some idea of where the waste might go, such as *to a big hole in the ground.* In the California group, 36% of the children described how waste is taken away in vehicles.

Figure 1. Four-year olds' ideas of creatures which live in polar areas

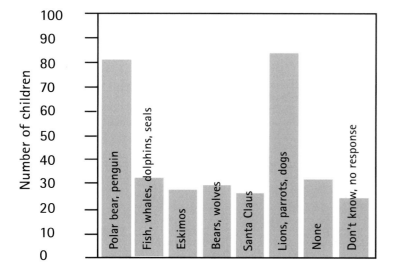

In both groups, around 20% of the children appeared to understand that waste can be separated into categories and treated in different ways. Of the children who could describe recycling, the majority said it meant that things are *made new again*. The most common misconception is that the same object is recycled as new, e.g. *the crisp packet is straightened out and filled up again*.

Sources of knowledge

Throughout the interviews, the researchers attempted to probe the sources of children's knowledge, in so far as it was possible to elicit meaningful answers. The three most frequently mentioned sources were TV (including video and film), family and direct experience (Figure 2). Interestingly, the learning experiences which came out best at promoting knowledge (TV and film) are not the same as those leading to understanding of issues (discussion with adults). Responses such as *I know all this 'cos I'm smart* were not uncommon, or very helpful!

Conclusions

The research demonstrates that very young children are capable of sophisticated thinking and reasoning about environmental issues. Many possess a good range of accurate scientific and ecological concepts (e.g. biodiversity and change) even before they start school. However, it is important for teachers to be aware that while such young learners may be good at recognising and naming unfamiliar creatures and landscapes, this does not necessarily mean they understand their context or existence. What is also clear is that some young children hold stereotypical ideas and misconceptions about people, places and issues which serve to filter the information they retain.

Some educators argue that ecological events are too far removed from children's experience to be suitable for the early years of schools. Yet the research sample shows that four-year olds are active thinkers in the realm of environmental issues, and are constantly trying to relate the ideas they encounter to their own experience. Around 20% of the four-year olds interviewed could appreciate that species are affected by long-term changes in the environment. Furthermore young children have a very real sense of care and concern for the world in which they are growing up. In short, they possess the knowledge, ideas and values which formal education can build upon in a sound and progressive way.

Further reading

Bell, P., Fisher, J., Baum, A. and Green, T. (1990) *Environmental Psychology*. Fort Worth: Holt, Rinehart and Winston.

Palmer, J. A. (1993) 'From Santa Claus to sustainability: emergent understanding of concepts and issues in environmental science', *International Journal of Science Education*, 15, 5.

Palmer, J. A. (1994) 'Acquisition of environmental subject knowledge in pre-school children: an international study' *Children's Environments*, 11, 3.

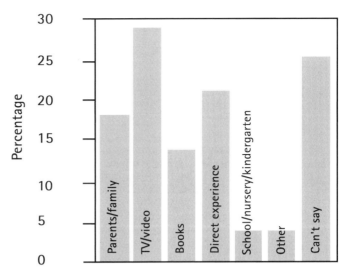

Palmer, J. A. (1995) 'Environmental thinking in the early years; understanding and misunderstanding of concepts relating to waste management', *Environmental Education Research*, 1, 1.

Palmer, J. A. and Suggate, J. (1996) 'Influences and experiences affecting the pro-environmental behaviour of educators', *Environmental Education Research*, 2, 1.

Palmer, J. A., Suggate, J. and Matthews, J. (1996) 'Environmental cognition: early ideas and misconceptions at the ages of four and six', *Environmental Education Research*, 2, 3.

Spencer, C., Blades, M. and Morsley, K. (1989) *The Child in the Physical Environment*. Chichester: John Wiley.

Tanner, T. (1980) 'Significant life experiences', *Journal of Environmental Education*, 11, 4, pp. 20-24.

Figure 2. Knowledge sources identified by four-year olds

Photo: Chris Garnett

Raising Awareness of Local Agenda 21

Peter Bloomfield

Until recently, environmental education was popular with primary school teachers. Now, with the pressures of the National Curriculum and the concentration on core subjects, it tends to be marginalised. However, Agenda 21 offers interesting opportunities (as illustrated by the research reported below) for integrating environmental education into all core and foundation subjects, especially geography.

Background

Many practitioners in primary, secondary and higher education are concerned about the changing local and global environment. Children are also concerned. This has been well documented by Chambers (1995) Neal and Palmer (1990) and SCAA (1996) (see also pages 30-31 and 32-33 in this book). However, a recent survey by WWF revealed that only 7% of schools in England and Wales had devised environmental policies (*Junior Education* news report, March 1995). This is worrying as it indicates a considerable lack in the breadth and balance of the curriculum.

In the 1992 Schumacher Lecture, Professor David Orr pointed out the enormous task facing future generations. In summary he maintained that:

> ... students of the next century will need to know how to create a civilisation that runs on sunlight, conserves energy, preserves biodiversity, protects soils and forests, develops sustainable local economies and restores the damage inflicted on the Earth.

We need to transform our schools and universities, he argued, in order to achieve these goals and promote ecological education.

Certainly there is an urgent need to audit current practice and plan a way forward. As identified elsewhere, 'much good work is already carried out in schools although litter collection and recycling is not enough. The underlying issues must be examined'. (Bloomfield, 1997)
The potential rewards are considerable:

Primary environmental education ... can help children develop a wide variety of economic, social, political, aesthetic and ethical perspectives; with the addition of scientific themes, it provides a broad perspective on the world. *Chambers, 1995*

Herein lies the crux of Local Agenda 21. It can be integrated across the whole curriculum through subjects and topics without detriment to any subjects and it can and should be rooted in the local community of the school.

Research methodology

Getting started
A telephone survey of head teachers in twelve primary schools in St Albans, Hertfordshire, established a personal link and secured permission for a full survey of all teaching and non-teaching staff in the schools involved. Head teachers suggested that staff be sent a brief note about Local Agenda 21 (LA21) before commencing the survey (Figure 1).

Conducting the survey
In the survey of teaching and non-teaching staff, 75% of the schools returned between one and thirteen surveys. Respondents were asked about their status and experience. Some schools are known to be predominantly 'middle class white' while others have up to 70% ethnic 'minority' pupils.

Involving the local authority
A brief interview was arranged with the Environment and Health Promotion Manager (EHPM) at St Albans District Council. At the time the Council had a vacancy for an Environment Co-ordinator whose job is to liaise with schools. The EHPM expressed the following views:

- Resources do not allow full contact with schools, although pupils visited the 'Environment Market' in 1996 and the Council receives pupil and school enquiries for local environmental data.

- The role of the co-ordinator will be to raise awareness of LA21 and environmental issues and to encourage school involvement in local projects.

- The role of the District Council is seen as providing links between schools and community groups. To assist this process the Council will facilitate the 'LA21 Forum' which has eighty member groups.

Schools are seen as a crucial link into LA21 and local environmental change.

What is Agenda 21?

A 'blueprint for action Agenda 21' was born at the Earth Summit in Rio de Janeiro in 1992. 'Local Agenda 21' is implemented by County and District councils and can be summarised as taking action locally to help resolve global problems.

There are four main strands for action:
- to decrease the use of raw materials and energy
- to reduce pollution and waste
- to protect fragile environments
- to share wealth and responsibilities more fairly in consideration of everyone's needs

Within the framework of LA 21 are the concepts of sustainability, values, attitudes and citizenship.

Figure 1. Teachers were provided with this brief description of Agenda 21

Outcomes

Most head teachers, while admitting they were not well informed about LA21 or the role of the local authority, were environmentally conscious, acknowledged its importance and welcomed discussions (Figure 2).

Teaching and non-teaching staff had opinions similar to head teachers but a few were environmentally active and, as a result, really well informed. Responses to this survey were encouraging considering it was conducted during the busy end of year period in July (Figure 3).

Concluding thoughts

The results of the research to date uphold the view that most schools are unaware of LA21 with respect to school/community links. However, while there appears to be a lack of specific policy and of awareness of the role of the local authority, 70% of the schools had a member of staff with responsibility for environmental education and there were plenty of examples that LA21 and environmental education were being delivered.

Both surveys indicated that geography and science were seen as the most common subjects for teaching these concepts, sometimes through topics, although good practice was evident where environmental education was cross-curricular or taught through PHSE. A high percentage of heads and classroom teachers welcomed the notion of external advice and practical help, possibly involving literacy and numeracy, in developing LA21 work.

A way forward

Acting as broker and negotiator the University of Hertfordshire plans to:
• run a workshop with head teachers (or co-ordinators) and the EHPM to discuss findings, share good practice, set targets and agree common aims

• deliver new courses to prepare student teachers by developing LA21/environmental education in a cross-curricular manner

• invite partnership school staff to join specific workshops run by visiting lecturers and workshop leaders from community groups as well as university subject specialists

• arrange student, school, community partnerships with students developing and leading a LA21 project in liaison with the head teachers

The research will span several years and the project will inform future work and continue within the BEd degree course. The aim is to involve new schools each year and to disseminate good practice through the university/school partnership network.

References

Bloomfield, P. (1998) 'The challenge of Agenda 21 at KS1, 2 and 3', *Geography*, 83, 2, in press.
Chambers, W. (1995) *Awareness into Action; Environmental Education in the Primary Curriculum*. Sheffield: Geographical Association.
Neal, P. and Palmer, J. (1990) *Environmental Education in the Primary School*. Oxford: Blackwell.
Orr, D. (1993) 'Schools for the twenty-first century', *Resurgence*, 160, October.
SCAA (1996) *Teaching Environmental Matters through the National Curriculum*. London: SCAA.

Results of Head Teacher Survey

• 100% did not have a LA 21 policy

• 92% did not have an environmental education policy (this *was* sometimes included in the development plan, geography or PHSE policy)

• 66% did not have a LA21/environmental education partnership within the community (many did have links with Groundwork Trust, Community Forest, Post Office etc.)

• 83% were not aware that the local authority should contact them about LA21

• 66% did have a member of staff with responsibility for environmental education (often within the role of geography or science co-ordinator)

• 42% integrated environmental education into curriculum planning; 50% did not

• 92% thought LA21/environmental education was best delivered through geography or science (one school named geography, history, science, art, IT and maths; another PHSE)

• 83% saw 'time' followed by 'curriculum overload' and 'resource provision' as the biggest constraints to delivering environmental education

• 83% would welcome advice and practical help in developing community links and working with the local university to that end

Figure 2. Results of survey of head teachers

Results of Survey of Teaching and Support Staff

• Length of experience of respondents: 1 to 39 years

• Responses mainly from teachers but included classroom assistants and one governor

• 80% plus were unaware of LA21, but some were highly informed

• 10% were involved in Friends of the Earth, Community Forest, LA21 forum, etc.

• Most thought environmental education was best taught through topics, e.g. local area, rainforest, local/distant locality studies, living in Britain; others thought best taught in school grounds, PHSE, science, geography, assemblies, nursery education. In one school 100% of respondents thought it best taught as a cross-curricular topic.

• Examples of good practice included:

recycling cans for cash linked with school
waste paper survey and community recycling
school grounds
pond and wildlife area
willow sculpture and habitat area
sensory exploration
local issues
quarrying, land use survey, habitats, pollution, erosion, traffic surveys, river surveys, role of local people (debate)
Green Finger Club
work linked with local and distant residential field trips

• 100% in some schools would welcome practical help in this area (some individuals declined due to lack of time or work overload)

Figure 3. Results of survey of teaching and non-teaching staff (57 responses)

Children's Ideas about Landscapes

*Michael Eyres
and Wendy Garner*

As children advance through the National Curriculum at key stages 1 and 2, they should be developing geographical knowledge, language and skills regarding the physical environment which will provide a sound basis for progression to key stage 3. Whether or not this is the case is investigated here through the medium of photographic interpretation.

Research background and context

In his book, *Primary Geography, Primary History*, Knight (1993) notes that the surprising thing about primary geography as a whole is how little it is researched. While many people have their own ideas about how it is taught and learned, their theories often lack any empirical basis. Only some 10% of 'geography education' articles in the British Education Index between 1986 and 1991 were research based, and only three consider how children interpret photographs.

Figure 1. An example of a photograph with questions What are these? How did they get here?

Photo: Sean Sprague, Panos Pictures

Regarding the use of photographs, Long (1953) found that ten-year old children were able to recognise and name certain features of the landscape. However, it appeared that they accepted landscape, represented photographically, as it is and did not show much curiosity as to the cause(s) of its formation. In more recent research, Stepans and Kuehn (1985) point out how developmental categories may affect children's responses. Two stages which are particularly significant are 'religious finalism' in which the child refers to supernatural causes such as God or angels, and 'true causality', where the child gives an accurate explanation of the physical phenomenon. In another paper, Walford and Haggett (1995) argue that the National Curriculum, by reasserting place studies, has enabled schools to re-establish physical geography as an equal partner to human geography. They quote from a 1993 postgraduate group, underlining the importance of physical geography and the study of landscape:

> The ultimate rationale for teaching geography has to be a simple one; to give future generations the opportunity to understand and appreciate the wonders of the space and place in which we live. (p. 12)

Research methodology

This study was carried out using an inductive approach in a school in a medium sized town. It involved 29 children aged five- to eleven-years old. The methodology is described below:

Stage 1 Photographs covering a range of different landforms were compiled (for example, mountains, streams, rivers and cliffs). Care was taken to use photographs of physical features which the children might have had contact with during their National Curriculum studies.

Stage 2 Photographs were mounted and set out, and questions about them were devised to form a structured interview (see Figure 1).

Stage 3 Interviews were carried out across the range of KS1 and KS2. The children were interviewed in pairs to make them feel more comfortable. Responses to the photographs were tape recorded and a written record was taken.

Stage 4 The interviews were transcribed and responses organised as follows:

1. For each landscape feature, a record was made of the number of children in each year group that
    a) recognised the feature,
    b) gave an alternative response,
    c) put forward no response at all.

2. With regard to physical processes, a record was kept of the key ideas put forward by each year group, and the number of children expressing each idea.

3. The ideas were graded as follows:
    A exhibits understanding
    B exhibits some understanding
    C exhibits response not relevant to the process/feature
    D no idea put forward

Research findings

Recognising features

The children showed strongest recognition of waterfalls (60% to 100% across the age range), mountains (80% to 100%), waves (75% to 100%) and seasonal clues (80% to 100%). Lakes were not readily recognised by KS1 children and understanding only increased moderately at KS2. The term 'coast' was not used by any of the children, but 'cliff' was increasingly recognised by years 5 and 6. There was confusion at all levels with regard to streams, rivers and valleys.

Understanding processes

The children exhibited a strong grasp of basic ideas about water and erosion, water catchment areas, coastal erosion and the seasons and a moderate understanding of the origins of streams. They were less confident about explaining mountain and valley formation, with many children suggesting that they were made by 'humans' or 'God'.

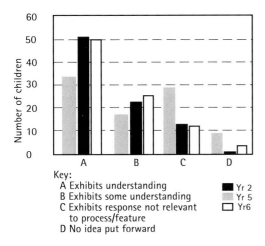

Key:
A Exhibits understanding
B Exhibits some understanding
C Exhibits response not relevant to process/feature
D No idea put forward

■ Yr 2
▨ Yr 5
☐ Yr6

Figure 2. Children's ideas about processes involved in landscape formation

Progression in Ideas

The results summarised in Figure 2 show a significant increase in the number of children in categories A and B from year 2 to year 6. They also show a decrease in responses which were inaccurate and a fall in category D between these years. Significantly, when looking at a photograph of *an island in the middle of a river* (described as such for the children), year 2 children speculated that *men kept digging, island made by men*, while by year 5 some of the children were saying *it was there already - bits of it were scooped away by the river* and *the river pushed through and left the island*.

Landscape vocabulary

As children learn about the physical landscape it is important to remember they are also grappling with specialist vocabulary (see pages 20-21). Working with a small group of children, York (1997) used photographs to explore children's perceptions of the difference between a hill and a mountain. Out of nine year 6 children, four said *a hill is composed of soil, whereas a mountain is composed of solid rock*, two thought the difference was related to shape (*mountains are pointed, but hills are round*) and only three saw size as relevant. York concluded:

this seems a natural assumption for children to reach when they are presented with stereotypical images of green hills and barren snow-capped mountains. With no formal teaching, these misconceptions are likely to prevail.

This is a significant finding because the landscape terms which are part of everyday speech also have a more precise geographical meaning. There is, for example, a big difference between a sea and an ocean but unless this is pointed out to them most primary school children think of them as synonymous (York, 1997).

Conclusions and implications for teachers

Asking children to interpret photographs seems a valid method for finding out the extent of their knowledge and understanding. The study showed that, although there was some confusion concerning the more difficult concepts, children's ideas about the physical environment appear to increase significantly as they develop and receive input through the National Curriculum. Their responses show that they are engaging with skills relating to the use of secondary sources and are using knowledge of processes to interpret 'clues' in the information, thus enabling them to arrive at geographically valid conclusions.

The findings of Stepans and Kuehn (1985) were found to relate to this study. For example, when children were unable to provide a reasoned explanation of a physical process (as in the case of mountain formation), they tended to revert to an alternative concept involving 'religious finalism' (e.g. mountains were put there by God).

Finally, the study lends weight to the argument put forward by Walford and Haggett (1995) that the National Curriculum has helped re-establish physical geography as a more equal partner to human geography. As a result children are now exposed to the basic concepts of physical geography by the end of KS2. This in turn can form the basis for success when they progress to secondary education. Clearly, in any review of the curriculum, it will be important to maintain the balance between physical and human geography.

References

Knight, P. (1993) *Primary Geography, Primary History*. London: David Fulton.

Long, M. (1953) 'Children's reactions to geographical pictures', *Geography*, 38.

Stepans, J. and Kuehn, C. (1985) 'Children's conceptions of the weather', *Science and Children*, September.

Walford, R. and Haggett, P.(1995) 'Geography and geographical education. Some speculations for the twenty-first century', *Geography*, 80, 1, pp. 3-13.

York, N. (1997) *Children's Conceptual Understanding of Landscape Features*. Unpublished dissertation. Canterbury Christ Church College.

Children's Ideas about Rivers
Trevelyan May

Since the word 'river' is in most children's vocabulary, it is easy to be misled into thinking that when they use it they have some shared understanding of its specialist meaning. But do they?

Research background

Piaget (1929), in questioning children about lakes and rivers, noted that their ideas develop through stages:

1 everything artificially made, the river bed, even the water: artificialism (to 7 or 8 years on average)
2 river bed dug out by people; water of natural origin: animism (to 9 or 10 years on average)
3 entirely natural

He emphasised how strongly *artificialism* is rooted in the children's minds. Associated with this is *animism*, attributing life and consciousness to the water.

Piaget (1930) also investigated children's explanations for the current in rivers, and identified stages:

1 the water (internal animist force) obeys people (external artificialist force) (to 7 or 8 years)
2 due to action of external force, stones, wind on water's internal spontaneous movement (8 or 9 years)
3 due to slope, a physical cause
4 due to slope and weight of water.

More recently Wilson and Goodwin (1981) have shown that children's concept of 'river' depends on their local experience and how near they live to a river.

Children's emerging concept of river was summarised by Wiegand (1993):
• Rivers are water
• Rivers are of considerable size
• The water moves
• A river moves along some course in its surroundings

Figure 1. Research methodology

Definitions - children write a definition of 'river' to reveal their understanding, from description to process, and to provide information for interview.

Word association - one-word responses to 'river', showing the links children make.

Drawing - an open, holistic activity, not constrained by the children's lack of geographical vocabulary, to reveal understanding they cannot convey in words, to reveal links between characteristics and process, and to allow the expression of feelings and attitudes.

Interview - discussing and annotating a photocopy of the child's drawing (not defacing the original), asking set questions and probing further (Figure 2).

Associated probes - name known rivers; sort photographs into 'river'/'not river', eliciting criteria applied.

Project

My project used a range of elicitation techniques (White and Gunstone, 1992) with a Year 5 class (9–10 years) in an urban school situated near a major Devon estuary, before the class undertook their river study. It was designed to see if children still have the ideas identified by Piaget. Although rivers and streams have become less visible in the urban landscape, increased travel and media exposure (TV and books) could have influenced children's thinking.

The stages used are shown in Figure 1. All the stages were trialled first in a pilot study, to refine the methodology.

Results

All the artificialist and animist ideas recorded by Piaget were included in the children's responses, and Wiegand's concept of progression was supported. The whole class had 'done' the water cycle in year 4, but only a few showed transference of ideas by indicating rain, slope, sea or evaporation and beginning to see the river as part of a system. The impact of local experience was clear, yet some surprising views were expressed by children living so close to a major river. For example, children living near the mouth of the estuary said *I've never been to the end of a river* and *at the end of the river there'd be a wall across.*

Children's definitions of 'river' included:
• wet water running down
• a long blue thing that's wet
• a thing with water in a long ditch
• something that flows and has fish and water
• a lot of water in a line
• something that runs through a hole
• a long tube shape full of water which is not man-made
• water that runs around a bank
• a long stream of water which has a long strong current which pulls everything along
• if you didn't have a river you probably wouldn't have any water between a valley

Most frequently mentioned in 31 responses were:

definitions of 'river'		word association	
water	31	water	22
movement	10	fish	14
shape	9	cold	12
contains things	9	wet	12
runs through a course	9	boat	10
		stone	9
		stream	6
		swim	6
		and 59 words mentioned by <6 children	

Their **drawings** were mostly plan views showing a predominantly rural setting with hills, wildlife and some recreational use. There were things in the water (fish, stones, boats, crabs etc.), and a common theme was a rounded source and mouth, or a funnel-shaped mouth.

Interviewing elicited that:
• The **water in the river comes from**: rain (13), sea (7), pipes (2), pond/lake (2), ditch (2), streams (1)

The **origin** of the channel is:
- *natural* (16): 'water rubbed away land'; 'the water is strong and it breaks away the land'; 'the river is heavy so it sunk in'
- *man-made* (11): mechanical diggers; 'men dug it out - all rivers start that way'; streams are smaller than rivers because 'they weren't dug so big'
- *both* natural and artificial (1)

Movement of the water is due to:
- wind (16); slope (7); 'water wants to' (1); doesn't move (1)

A river **starts**:
- hills (5), sea (5), land (4), pond/lake (4), wall (2), waterfall (2), sewer (2), drains (1)

A river **ends**:
- sea (20), land (3), wall (2), sand (1), don't know

Associated probes

The Nile was the most **frequently named** river, followed by the local river and the Thames.

The **criteria** used to sort the photographs were:
- **River** big; long; meanders; in a natural (rural) setting
- **Not-river** 'too small'; has signs of human intervention (rubbish, walls).

Some children contradicted the artificialist perspective they had expressed previously.

Implications for teaching

One should develop children's graphicacy skills by looking into photographs of rivers in a variety of localities. Children need to see rivers in urban as well as rural settings (Figures 3 and 4). Asked if rivers go through towns, children replied:

Little streams can, but not sure about rivers, think they can't.

Yes, in different countries: Italy, France - don't know about England.

Could have houses at the back of the grass.

When engaged in urban and rural river fieldwork, some children believe that what they see in front of them is the whole river - how do they distinguish a river from a lake? They must be helped to extend this 'picture-postcard' or framed view. Drawing their attention to the flow, and asking questions such as *Where's the water coming/flowing from?*, *Where's it flowing to?*, *Why is this happening?* will encourage them to extend their perspective and their thinking. The use of aerial and other photographs and maps in conjunction with fieldwork is essential here; for example, sequencing a set of photographs of a river from source to mouth, and matching them to localities marked on a map.

Even children with some understanding of the water cycle and the place of rivers within it still invoke artificialism and animism in their explanations. As Piaget showed, it's during KS 2 that most children can be expected to accept natural explanations. To do this they need experience of rivers through fieldwork and secondary sources.

References

Piaget, J. (1929) *Child's Conception of the World*. London: Routledge & Kegan Paul.

Piaget, J. (1930) *Child's Conception of Causality*. London: Routledge & Kegan Paul.

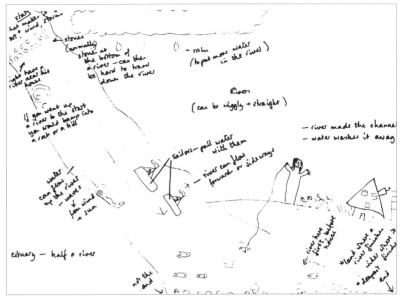

Figure 2. Typical drawing, annotated by researcher

White, R. and Gunstone, R. (1992) *Probing Understanding*. Lewes: Falmer Press.

Wiegand, P. (1993) *Children and Primary Geography*. London: Cassell.

Wilson, P. and Goodwin, M. (1981) 'How do twelve- and ten-year-old students perceive rivers?', *Geographical Education* pp. 5-16.

Figures 3 and 4. Rivers in rural and urban settings

Photo: Antony Wilkinson

Photo: PhotoAir

Child's Eye View of Cities

Helen Baldwin and Miles Opie

Children readily use the words village, town, city, but what meaning do they give to them, and how do they perceive the settlements? As student teachers in East Devon some of our school experience is in small village schools, so we thought it would be interesting to explore rural children's perceptions of urban areas. For children living in a village, is the city a place of wonder, fear, or merely of visits?

Previous research

Lynch (1960) talked about the 'legibility' of a city, by which he meant the ease with which its features can be recognised and organised into a coherent pattern or structure. How legible are cities to children? There have been studies of children's perception and understanding of their own area but, as far as we could ascertain, none of rural children's ideas about urban areas, or vice versa.

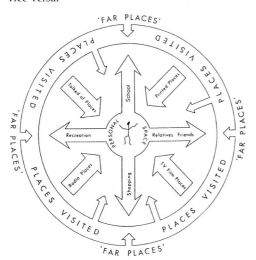

Figure 1. The child in information space (Goodey, 1973)

Figure 2. Sources of spatial information (Matthews, 1992). Each link aids the formation of a concept or image of the place - in this case, a city

Goodey (1973) and Matthews (1992) presented diagrammatically the direct and indirect experiences that help form children's perceptions of place (Figures 1 and 2). Although the process by which children develop a concept of place is fascinating, our studies focused more on children's feelings about cities and the concepts they hold, not on how they acquired them.

Methodology

We carried out our studies in year 3/4 classes in village schools some 40 kilometres from the nearest city and 16 kilometres from the nearest town. We used a wide range of elicitation techniques (White and Gunstone, 1992) including word association, definitions, picture sorting, children talking about their experiences of cities, drawing (part of) a city, interviews about drawing, and concept mapping, requiring the children to consider 'city' in terms of form, function, quality of life and of environment, and to express their feelings and attitudes.

Findings

Individuals construct their own meanings and often formulate different and contradictory ideas about the same phenomena, and their ideas often seem peculiar from a teacher's point of view - described by Driver *et al.* (1985) as 'incoherent ideas'. We found many contradictions; children's responses to the picture activity often contradicted their concept map or their drawing and interview. But generally the children had an understanding of what a city is like: a big place containing large buildings, crowds of people, many shops and roads full of cars; a noisy, polluted place with little greenery, space or wildlife. The strongest city image was of skyscrapers. These are expressions of the stereotypical images drawn from books, television and film. Some are also images experienced directly by the children during visits to cities (Figure 3).

The children in our study:
- considered towns to be much less 'built up' than cities, with more open spaces, more green and less pollution, while shopping facilities are seen as important in both
- indicated rather negative images when talking about 'city' - pollution, overcrowding, crime and large buildings, factories and skyscrapers rather than housing
- think that 'foreign' countries do not have cities. They used the word 'foreign' as a synonym for 'less developed', and did not consider New York, Madrid or Paris to be in 'foreign' countries
- tended to believe that cities are inhabited by 'only rich people and tramps', 'shopkeepers' or 'no-one'
- had begun to identify an idea of the city - town - village hierarchy

Overall we found that a majority of the children had visited a city at least once. Unsurprisingly, their comprehension was fairly superficial, exposed by interview and by the photograph sorting exercise. They did not appreciate:
- the wide cross-section of people living in cities
- the diversity of size and form of different cities
- that poorer nations have cities

Not unexpectedly they held a western perspective. The children did not fear the city, nor were they enthused to live in a city due to the perceived crowding, noise and fumes.

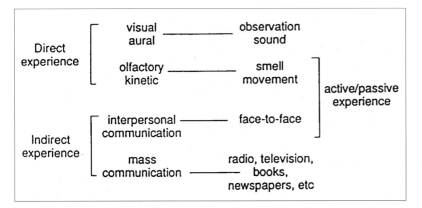

Implications for teaching

We think it is important to first establish children's ideas, then challenge them with experiences in conflict with their expectations, encouraging them to reconsider–i.e. to adopt a constructivist approach.

Children's understanding of places 'is the result of a complex relationship between development in the cognitive and affective domains' (Wiegand, 1992). Direct as well as indirect experience, including mapwork and the use of diagrams and pictures, is essential in developing a child's understanding of settlements - in this case, the city. But as Ward (1990) pointed out, a child's view of the city is at a lower level or viewpoint than an adult's, so a child will notice different things:

ADULTS notice functional aspects: bank, car park, road system
CHILDREN notice people, animals, birds, vegetation, natural phenomena

In a city there is too much for a child to take in. Children remember places through association and feelings, through attraction or repulsion; a building because it was spooky, a cafe because it sold nice ice cream, a park by climbing a tree.

The children's images of cities were largely negative, so the positive aspects need to be emphasised. Children accept that shops are a prominent feature of cities, but do not appreciate that many people live there, so visits should include not just the commercial centres (the CBDs - central business districts) but also residential areas and industrial zones. In other words, children should start to map land-use. They can recognise areas of Victorian terraced houses, post-war semis, tower blocks and modern estates, and their relationship to the centre of the city; this will help them towards an understanding of the structure of urban areas. Transects of the main routes, from outskirts to centre, would contribute to this.

The western bias of most of the children could be redressed by using urban 'distant locality' resource packs, not just the rural packs. Children rejected Lima as a city because the photograph showed shanty towns and poor people - 'you don't find poor people in a city' (which contradicted the view expressed that tramps live in cities!). As well as all this cognitive work, children should be encouraged to consider and express their feelings.

References

Driver, R. et al. (1985) Children's Ideas in Science. Open University.
Goodey, B. (1973) Perceptions of the Environment. University of Birmingham.
Lynch, K. (1960) The Image of the City, Cambridge Mass.: MIT Press.
Matthews, H.M. (1992) Making Sense of Place. Hemel Hempstead: Harvester Wheatsheaf.
Ward, C. (1990) The Child in the City. London: Architectural Press.
White, R. and Gunstone, R. (1992) Probing Understanding. Lewes: Falmer Press.
Wiegand, P. (1992) Places in the Primary School. Lewes: Falmer Press.

Children's predominant images of cities

BIG
- there are lots of facilities in the city, more than in towns and villages
- cities are big, popular places
- a city is a big, noisy place with lots of shops and people
- a city is a very big town with lots of big shops and buses

BUSY
- lots of people, overcrowded, traffic jams
- a city is a busy place
- you have to push through everyone to get anywhere
- skyscrapers, cars and so many people that the cars can't move

CATHEDRAL
- usually in cities because cities are bigger and have more space

CRIME
- more than in towns and villages, lots of robberies
- robbers and things because it is a big city and no-one cares what is going on

CROWDED
- not enough room with small houses so more have to be built to fit everyone in

FEW TREES
- not many around the shops

HOMELESS
- people from towns who have moved to the city to get shelter because there are not many walkways in towns
- because there are so many people and no more room to build

HOMES
- people live on the outskirts and work in the middle, they don't want to live where they work
- when people aren't working they spend their time going home

LIVING
- can't sleep, too noisy
- hard to find the building you need
- interesting

NASTY
- people get sick from the dirt and everything, especially in the busy ones

NOISY
- from cars, children shouting, birds singing loudly and ducks quacking on the river

POLLUTION
- there are not many trees because of pollution (smoke) from cars and factories
- noise
- people aren't as healthy because of dirt, fog and smog (car exhausts and smoke mixed with fog)
- from oil, coke cans and litter, and smoke from cars
- from cars, traffic, factory fumes, machinery and acid

SMELLY
- from rubbish bins and stuff being kicked over

TRAVEL
- people travel by bus because they need the space for other things
- they would rather use the space to build places for people to work

Figure 3. Children's images of cities based on quotations and responses from all survey methods

41

The European Dimension

John Halocha

Learning about Europe can promote children's ideas of citizenship and international understanding. It can also serve to develop a wide range of geographical skills including mapwork and the ability to use IT. The research project described here was carried out over a three year period. It revealed that teachers who have made study visits to Europe are able to use this knowledge and experience extremely effectively in the classroom. Penpals and school-to-school links are also valuable ways of enhancing learning.

Research context

The research was carried out in an Oxfordshire primary school which has developed a strong European dimension within its curriculum during the last three years. Staff have made many exchange study visits and established links with schools in a number of European countries. A wide range of geographical resources has been

Figure 1. Teachers explain photos they took on study trips

Photo: John Halocha

created involving geographical enquiries and the use of IT. The emphasis has been to base learning on direct links with children and teachers in other countries, rather than relying on published materials. Convery's (1997) research raises interesting ideas about how children begin to understand ideas and information relating to other European countries. In order to extend this understanding, it was decided to focus on the way different resources can enhance children's geographical comprehension of Europe.

Research methodology

Observations and interviews with teachers and children over the last three years provided background evidence for the study. Teaching resources were also carefully examined along with children's work and the exchange materials sent between schools. More detailed data were collected from 54 children in year 5 and 6 classes. At the end of the project the children were encouraged to discuss in small informal groups what they had learned about other European countries. These discussions were tape recorded. The children were also given simple writing and drawing tasks to encourage them to remember and talk about their ideas.

Findings

Teachers' personal experiences and the quality of resources they collect

Teachers' own experiences appeared to have the greatest impact on children's learning. A number of the school staff had made study visits to other European countries, funded by the Comenius and Lingua schemes. These visits gave them the opportunity to get to know their partner schools and learn about the surrounding locality in great depth. At the same time they were able to collect many teaching resources.

In their interviews many of the children commented on how much they had learnt about the country they were studying by listening to their teacher talking and being able to ask direct questions. This understanding was reinforced by the range of resources which the teachers had assembled. For example, one class discussed the land use shown in a photograph of a Spanish town (Figure 1). As well as visiting the locality, the teachers had considered the questions that children might ask back in England. One child remarked: *We can't ask a book what its pictures really show, but we can ask our teacher.*

The children also made comments about the value of up-to-date resources. If they wanted the latest information, they could obtain it from their link school. A Spanish property paper, for example, encouraged the children to look carefully at building materials, the demands of the climate and the way of life of people in the locality. This work provided opportunities to develop key geographical skills.

The teachers were also able to help children interpret the resources and see the possible links between them. In one case a set of photographs was related to a map and key geographical skills developed from them. Some children raised the issue of stereotyping and the problem of only getting one point of view. They believed that their teachers would probably give them a more balanced picture of life in another country than they would get from books. However, this does place considerable responsibility on teachers who make study visits and raises the issue of how balanced any view of another country might be.

Resources created by children

The children identified the wide range of magazines, faxes and project materials which were exchanged between the various countries as the second most valuable source of information (Figure 2). These provided a great deal of interest

and discussion. Again, the children remarked on how these resources gave recent information on life in other places. Some also commented that because they had had to produce similar materials to send abroad to their link school, they were beginning to think about the balance and accuracy of the information they received. This line of thinking has excellent potential for exploring questions of bias.

Figure 2. The children in an Italian school provided a range of materials about their area. The caption to their drawing translates: 'We live in Camerano. Camerano is a village situated on a hill with a lot of countryside around it'

Photo: John Halocha

43

Penpals

The project gave the children a chance to make penpals (Figure 3). In the evaluation the children listed many examples of how they had learnt about other people and places through these links. Everyday life and families were the main themes. The majority of comments concentrated on the similarity between their penpals and families to people in this country. The children accepted that their new friends spoke other languages, ate different foods and had various traditions, but were really the same underneath. The majority of the class felt it was very interesting to be able to ask questions and get replies. The most common complaint was how long some penpals took to reply and how disappointing it was if no reply came at all. The success of many European links comes from making personal contacts of this kind. If such work can be developed, important aspects of citizenship and cross-cultural understanding could be built into the primary curriculum.

Holidays and personal experiences

Not all the children's ideas about Europe came from school resources. Two thirds of the group had visited other European countries and declared that holidays were a 'good way to see what goes on in those places'. These remarks were probed in depth. The most common learning experiences concerned food, transport, shops, buildings, how people dressed and what the weather was like. Some of the children admitted that they only saw a holiday-maker's view of a country but the majority felt they were seeing everyday life. This could be a valuable resource for teachers to develop. For example, more children had visited France than any other country. When they talked about where they had been, some children began to question their earlier impressions. One child who declared that France was '*well, big but it's mountains all over*' qualified his ideas when other children talked about the flat parts they had seen. If teachers are able to build on these European holiday experiences, they may be able to develop children's geographical understanding using first hand experience.

Visiting teachers from other countries

Teachers from the partner schools involved in the Comenius project visited England and worked with the children on a range of activities. Interestingly, the children did not mention this at

Figure 3. The continental children sent 'self-portraits' to their English penpals

all. Even when prompted they found it hard to remember what had happened and could not explain why. Possibly language proved a barrier. Also, as the school had many visitors, the children may have been confused. The implications here are that schools need to prepare pupils for such visits in order to make the most of them. Adult to adult links appear to be effective in resource creation and policy development, but the role of a visiting adult needs careful planning.

Classroom implications

Teaching about Europe (and indeed distant places in other parts of the world) is a valuable way of developing geographical skills and understanding. European funding and the facilities of organisations such as the Central Bureau can enable teachers to develop a range of resources and experiences. These can have a considerable impact on children's knowledge, skills and understanding. Equally teachers can build on and extend the personal travel experiences which children bring to school. Effective planning will help to ensure that this important aspect of the primary school

curriculum is developed to its full potential.

References and further reading

Bell, G. H. (1991) *Developing a European Dimension in Primary Schools*. London: David Fulton.

Central Bureau for Educational Visits and Exchanges (1991) *Making the Most of your Partner School Abroad*. London: Central Bureau.

Convery, A. (1997) *Pupils' Perceptions of Europe: Identity and Education*. London: Cassell.

Halocha, J. W. (1997) 'The European dimension in primary education' in Tilbury, D. and Williams, M. (eds) *Teaching and Learning Geography*. London: Routledge.

Wiegand, P. (1992) *Places in the Primary School*. Lewes: Falmer Press.

For information on making links in Europe and teacher study visits, contact:

The Central Bureau for Educational Visits and Exchanges
10 Spring Gardens
London SW1A 2BN
Tel: 0171 389 4004

Teaching About Distant Places

Vicki Harrington

Children's images of and attitudes towards other countries and the people living there are of great importance in the modern multi-cultural and interdependent world. Geography is uniquely placed to challenge stereotypes and help children build up accurate and unbiased images. It would appear that this is best undertaken at an early age before ideas become entrenched.

Research background

We receive so much information that we try to process it in a simple way by putting it into categories. Stereotypes, according to Tajfel (1969), are a special form of categorisation. They are over-generalised beliefs which are often applied to people and may develop into racial prejudice. Once firmly established, they are difficult to dislodge.

Research indicates that children are aware of their racial identity from an early age. Aboud (1988) argues that children as young as four express negative reactions to certain ethnic groups. However, these ideas are superficial and relatively easy to change. Indeed it appears that children learn and repeat them just as they would any other fact.

As children grow older their ideas become more entrenched. In a small-scale student study, Friend (1995) found that six-year olds changed their images of Africa as a result of a short teaching programme, while ten-year olds tended to retain negative attitudes. By secondary school age stereotypes are even harder to shift. Marsden (1976) discusses the difficulty of breaking down 'attitudinal rigidity' while Hibberd (1983) notes that, in a longitudinal study of 3 000 American students, their impressions of Africa hardly altered between the ages of 12 and 17 despite a carefully structured course on the Third World.

It would appear then that stereotypes need to be challenged and modified at an early age. However, Binns (1979) and Knight (1993) both argue that for teaching to be effective it is essential first to establish how pupils perceive the world, and that 'concept modification' must take children's existing ideas into account.

Methodology

There are very few studies on the effects of teaching in reducing stereotypes. With this in mind a research project was set up to see how children's images and ideas of Africa changed as a result of a balanced teaching programme (Figure 1). The research was conducted with 28 children in a year 4 and 5 class in a Kent primary school. All the pupils were white and of English origin apart from one Indian child who had lived in this country from the age of three. None of them had been taught about Africa before.

Over a nine week period the children found out about rich and poor areas of Nairobi. Most of the information for the project came from an Action Aid photopack *Nairobi, Kenyan City Life*. A large stimulus display provided an invaluable additional resource. The display changed and developed as the project progressed and was used to prompt discussion.

To begin with, the children collected facts and figures about Kenya and extracted information from maps and atlases. They then used the photographs and other material in the pack to focus on the locality of Kariobangi. The children made comparisons between London and Nairobi and discussed their images and stereotypes. Rich and poor areas within Nairobi were also contrasted using maps and photographs. Finally the children found out about the daily life of people living in Kariobangi which they compared with their own timetable and routines. This helped to highlight the way certain things, such as food, clothes and shelter, are needed by people all over the world.

The children were tested before and after the project using four different methods:
1. *Word Associations* - a brainstorm in which the children wrote down all the words that came into their heads.

2. *Pictures* - the children were asked to draw pictures showing clothes, houses and food.

3. *Word Pairs* - the children were given a grid with a set of positive and negative words arranged in pairs and asked to record their ideas (see Oppenheim, 1992).

4. *Word Cards* - the children were given 20 cards, each with a different descriptive word on it, and asked to assign them to boxes labelled Africa, England, Both, Nobody (after Davey, 1983).

The decision to use a wide variety of research techniques was taken quite deliberately. Steadman (1982) stresses that a wide range of methods is likely to give a more realistic picture of children's ideas and that it is best not to rely exclusively on one approach.

Figure 1. Drawings showing what the children thought about Africa before they began the project

Results

One of the questions that emerges from this study is whether travel affects children's images. A quarter of the children had never visited a foreign country, half had visited either one or two. The results of the word association exercise present a conflicting picture; some of the children who had travelled abroad had a more positive image of Africa but others did not. The children who had not travelled so widely had a range of positive and negative images. Research with such a limited number of children has to be treated with caution but there is no real evidence from the sample studied to suggest that travel within western Europe makes children more sympathetic to distant cultures.

Conclusion

While the class teacher may be able to have a positive influence on children's attitudes and values, at the end of the day children return to homes where parental influence may be negative. It is important for children to be taught about distant lands in a positive way at school, right through the primary years. The absence of any requirement to teach children about distant lands at KS1 is a serious omission; and whilst at KS2 children have to study a distant locality there is no reference to teaching attitudes and values.

Geography from 5-16 (1986) suggests that one of the objectives of primary school geography is to develop positive attitudes to other countries and their peoples to counteract 'racial and cultural stereotyping and prejudice' (p. 11). The working group which wrote the first version of the Geography National Curriculum (DES, 1990) also argues that pupils should be sensitive to the attitudes and values of people in different places.

The question is, how can we afford to leave these areas out of the geography curriculum in view of the increasing body of research evidence on how stereotypes and negative attitudes develop?

Before Project	After Project
1. Word Associations	
The children appeared to have a great number of shared images of Africa. More than 70% of the class used words such as elephants and desert/sand. Every child mentioned that Africa was hot and sunny and none of them made reference to a contrasting type of environment. These highly stereotypical images correspond with the findings of Graham and Lynn (1989).	Images of elephants, hot weather and the desert still appear to be strong but a greater variety of images is also evident, with some children mentioning cities alongside deserts and trees. Black people feature less often, supporting the views of Stratta (1989) and Bale (1986) that teaching can reduce, but not necessarily eliminate, stereotypes.
2. Pictorial Representations	
Sixty per cent of the children thought Africans would live in houses made of straw, mud or twigs, because they could not afford anything else. Images of poverty and illness also featured when the children drew a person of their own age. The drawings of food often conveyed a hunter gatherer image with coconuts featuring prominently.	The children continued to draw pictures showing different aspects of poverty. However they also made drawings of wealthy houses, large high rise buildings and busy city streets. These more sophisticated images tended to predominate.
3. Word Pairs	
Sixty eight per cent of the children held negative attitudes towards the country while only 32% held negative attitudes towards the people. This could be a reflection of the sympathy children naturally feel for others.	Comments about the country indicate a relatively even balance between positive and negative images, while comments about the people are almost wholly positive.
4. Word Cards	
Only about a quarter of the children assigned positive comments to the African group while nearly all of them made positive comments about the English group.	The positive comments are now more evenly distributed between the African and English groups. Generally the children are much less willing to assign positive or negative images to one group in preference to another, reflecting a more mature attitude.

Figure 2. Children's images and attitudes before and after the project

References and further reading

Aboud, F. (1988) *Children and Prejudice.* Oxford: Blackwell.

Bale, J. (1986) *Geography in the Primary School.* London: Routledge.

Binns, J. A. (1979) 'How we see "them"', *Teaching Geography,* 4, pp. 176-177.

Davey, A. (1983) in Aboud, F. (1988) *Children and Prejudice.* Oxford: Blackwell.

DES (1986) *Geography from 5 to 16: Curriculum Matters.* London: HMSO.

Friend, C. (1995) *Can Positive Attitudes be Developed Towards Economically Developing Countries in the Primary Phase?* Unpublished dissertation. Canterbury Christ Church College.

Graham, J. and Lynn, S. (1989) 'Mud huts and flints: children's images of the Third World', *Education 3-13,* June, pp. 29-32.

Hibberd, D. (1983) 'Children's images of the third world', *Teaching Geography,* 9, 2.

HMI (1986) *Geography from 5-13 (Curriculum Matters 7).* London: HMSO.

Katz, D. and Zalk, S. (1978) 'Modification of children's racial attitudes', *Developmental Psychology,* 14, pp. 447-461.

Knight, P. (1993) *Primary Geography, Primary History.* London: David Fulton.

Marsden, W. E. (1976) 'Stereotyping and Third World geography', *Teaching Geography,* 1, 5.

Oppenheim, A. N. (1992) *Questionnaire Design and Attitude Measurement.* Oxford: OUP.

Steadman, S. (1982) 'Evaluation techniques' in McCormick, R. (ed) *Calling Education to Account.* London: Heinemann.

Stratta, E. (1989) 'First year juniors and cultural diversity', *Education 3-13 ,* June, pp. 21-27.

Tajfel, H. (1969) in Wiegand, P. (1992) *Places in the Primary School.* Lewes: Falmer Press.

Using Globes

John Sharp

To understand globes is to understand something of the nature of the Earth itself. Just how well can this be achieved throughout the primary years? A recent research project carried out by the author is described here.

Introduction

Although there has been considerable research into children and maps (Catling, 1996) and children and the environment (Matthews, 1992), we know surprisingly little about children and globes. By this I do not mean there is a lack of suggestions for classroom activities which involve globes. I mean there is very little research which informs us of how children learn about globes, what they learn from them, and when best to use them.

One of the reasons for this lack of interest is that Piagetian theories of child development suggest that young children find it hard to comprehend abstract concepts. Another is that many teachers are themselves uncertain of the background knowledge and ideas needed to support a suitable teaching programme. Yet there are plenty of possible activities. These include a comparison of globes and atlas maps, place studies, work on routes and journeys and the study of global environmental issues. Such work, of course, satisfies many of the requirements of the Geography National Curriculum which specifically requires children to use and interpret globes at KS2.

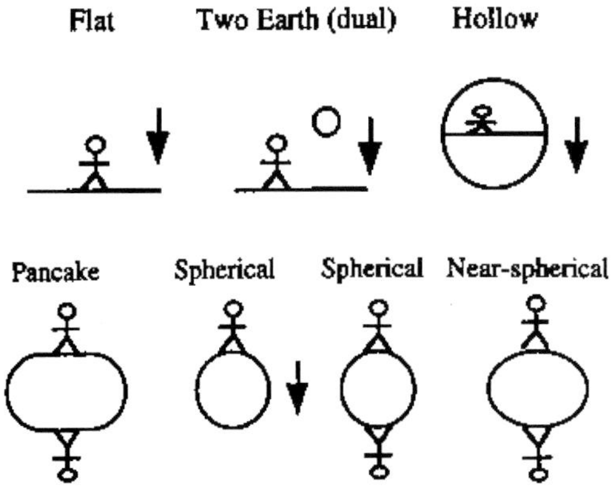

Figure 1. Children's 'models' of the Earth in space. Learning may proceed in steps or jumps and not necessarily from left to right. Arrows indicate gravity acts 'down'. (After Nussbaum, 1985 and Vosniadou and Brewer, 1992)

The Earth in space

All of us who have taught in primary schools know that children bring their own ideas about things to school - ideas which have been influenced by many kinds of experiences. As a result, their notions often differ from those of informed adults while nevertheless making perfect sense within a given context. Such ideas are 'alternative' and notoriously difficult to change. Children's ideas about the Earth in space provide perfect examples and have been investigated by a number of different researchers (Nussbaum, 1985; Vosniadou and Brewer, 1992).

The Earth is a near-spherical body of considerable size with a gravitational attraction that keeps our feet firmly on the ground wherever we stand. However, many children, particularly those coming to school for the first time, think that the Earth is as it appears, i.e. 'flat', and argue that it is impossible to live anywhere other than 'on top' of it. Other 'models' have also been described. Some children believe that two Earths exist, 'ours', and the one they hear about which is 'somewhere else'. Some think the Earth hollow and consisting of two hemispheres, one solid, one the sky. The Earth is even thought of as being like a 'pancake' - thick and 'flat' but round at the sides (Figure 1). While working with globes is certainly possible for children holding any of the Earth 'models' described above, meaningful learning and understanding can only be achieved when something of the nature of the Earth itself has been, or is in the process of being, grasped.

Research project

A recent study conducted by the author investigated children's ideas about the Earth in space. Fifty children from a Devon primary school were involved, drawn equally from a year 2 (top infant) and year 6 (top junior) class. All had undertaken work on the Earth's shape, the distribution of continents and oceans, and similarities and differences between a globe and the 'real' Earth.

Most of the research involved largely structured interviews administered on a one-to-one basis (Figure 2). Readers are encouraged to try this procedure for themselves but should avoid shortcuts as children give responses which are difficult to interpret in isolation. Drawings provided another approach. These tended to highlight the variation within and between year groups (interpretation and visualisation of what is to be drawn, 3D-2D transposition, spatial representation) and were particularly useful for assessment and differentiation (Figure 3). Place details were not actually considered in the context of the task presented, but could be studied later (see pages 10-11 and 50-51 in this book).

Findings

Findings from the research are set out in Figure 4. As this shows, nearly all the year 2 children (84%) thought the Earth was spherical, as did 23 children in year 6. Two children in year 6 actually described the Earth as near-spherical (advanced). In year 2, sixteen of the children had an extended 'model' of the Earth which included drawings showing land masses and in year 6 this

Figure 4. Comparison of year 2 and year 6 children

Notion	Year 2 (25 children)	Year 6 (25 children)
Earth is spherical	21	25
Aware of effect of gravity	13	19
Earth is a planet	8	23
Earth is part of solar system	23	25

R: What shape is the Earth?

J: It's sort of an oval.

R: Is there a shape here that's most like the Earth? (Selection of 2D and 3D shapes shown on a tray.)

J: Well ...not really, that one if it was a bit flatter, it's flat there and flat there (referring to opposite ends of a sphere).

R: How do people know it's that shape?

J: Well ...it's in all the books that I've read and when I went to this museum ...it's not really round, it's a round oval shape.

R: Imagine for now that you're in a rocket. Can you draw a picture of what the Earth might look like from space?

J: (Draws a shape like an oval with recognisable land masses.) It's got like sort of like clouds on it, there's Asia, Africa and India coming down there. It's 'cause we were here in Dammam in Saudi Arabia when I saw it. And that was it really. That's us (referring to the UK).

R: What colour would the Earth be?

J: Well ...it'd look green but sometimes it would be browny and yellow, the sea would be blue and sometimes green but because of the atmosphere you'd only see clouds and that.

R: What would you expect to see all around the Earth? (Uses Jennifer's drawing to point.)

J: Well...what we'd see would be the Moon there, a big Sun there...planets.

R: How come we can't see the Earth's 'roundness' when we look out of the window there (uses Jennifer's drawing and choice of shape to illustrate 'roundness')?

J: It's too big to see it all.

R: Where do people live on the Earth?

J: They don't live on the sea unless they've got a houseboat. They live in Africa, Asia, India, Saudi Arabia...all over really...in towns...not deserts or cold areas. China has a huge population.

R: Have you ever heard of anybody falling off the Earth?

J: No.

R: Could anybody ever fall off the Earth?

J: No...because of gravity. [Gravity?] Well...it's because we call New Zealand upside down 'cause we're here and they're down there...it's hard to put it...how I'd explain it to my mum is like this ...if you're in a plane and flying to Australia or to Africa or anywhere that's there you wouldn't feel the plane going upside down...they're just on a different point of the Earth.

R: What is the Earth?

J: The Earth is just like another planet but people live there. Other planets like because of the different atmospheres well...nobody could live on Mars but if you stood on there it's too hot...it depends on where you are from the Sun.

R: Do you recognise any of the objects in these pictures (Sun, Moon and planets shown)?

J: (Identifies everything but the Moon.)

Figure 2. Interview with Jennifer aged 10 years 11 months.
(R=Researcher; J = Jennifer)
Jennifer's responses are quite detailed for her age, though not uncommon, and can be considered in terms of the language used, the logic and reasoning involved, the geographical content, and so on. She appears to hold an advanced, near-spherical 'model' but still retains some 'alternative'

Year 2	7	3	3	9	2	1	0
Year 6	0	0	1	10	7	5	2

Figure 3. Children's freehand sketches of the Earth in space showed a clear progression from year 2 to year 6. Figures represent the number of examples in each year

was the case for all 25 children. In year 2, one child appeared to imagine the Earth as conforming to the pancake-like 'model', another to the dual or two-Earth 'model', and two had ideas which could not be classified at all.

Conclusion and research agenda

This study clearly demonstrates the value of teaching children about globes. It seems that infants can understand a great deal about the shape of the Earth and its position in space. The common notion that children are 'incapable' of understanding such abstract ideas needs to be questioned.

The implications for primary geography and geographical education are far reaching. By observing and reporting on how children work with globes of different sorts and in various contexts, teachers have an ideal opportunity to become involved in the research process as well as helping themselves and others to monitor, evaluate, and improve their own practice.

However, much work still remains to be done on establishing the importance of globes and how globework skills and concepts develop.

References

Catling, S. (1996) 'Technical interest in curriculum development: a programme of map skills' in Williams, M. (ed) *Understanding Geographical and Environmental Education: The Role of Research*. London: Cassell, pp. 93-111.

Matthews, M. H. (1992) *Making Sense of Place: Children's Understanding of Large Scale Environments*. Hemel Hempstead: Harvester Wheatsheaf.

Nussbaum, J. (1985) 'The Earth as a cosmic body' in Driver, R., Guesne, E. and Tiberghien, A. (eds) *Children's Ideas in Science*. Buckingham: Open University Press, pp. 171-192.

Vosniadou, S. and Brewer, W. F. (1992) 'Mental models of the earth: a study of conceptual change in childhood', *Cognitive Psychology*, 24, pp. 535-585.

Understanding the World Map

Patrick Wiegand

The National Curriculum has focused attention on children's global place knowledge. Yet we have little evidence of how children think about the world as a whole or of their understanding of the relationship between the spherical Earth and a flat world map. What is described here is a series of linked investigations into children's developing awareness of the size and shape of the continents and how they 'fit' together. What underlies these studies is the belief that, if we can find out more about common classroom misconceptions, we can devise more effective teaching strategies to enable children to have a more accurate and durable frame of reference for their developing store of locational knowledge.

Drawing, identifying, arranging and sticking

Unpacking children's thinking about the Earth's land masses is complex and so several complementary methodologies were used.

1. **Sketch maps** 268 children aged from 5 to 11 were asked to draw a free-recall sketch map of the world on a sheet of A4 paper, under individual supervision and with no reference to maps or globes.

2. **Globe drawings** In a separate study, 72 children aged from 8 to 11 drew the outline of the continents on 'blank' surrogate globes made by spraying cheap plastic footballs with blue paint. The spherical drawings were done with black washable felt tip pen and afterwards transferred to a flat sheet of paper using a specially designed 'map projection'. This was based on a diamond shaped 'graticule' formed by stretching a small nylon bag over the football.

3. **Card shapes** In a further study, 52 children from 10 to 11 were invited to identify and arrange laminated card continent shapes in the form of a world map. The results were compared with those from a task in which a similar set of self-adhesive green vinyl shapes had to be arranged on a 'blank' blue globe.

4. **Comparing continents** Finally, 62 children aged 11 to 12 were asked to identify a set of continent cut-out shapes and then estimate the size of each continent in relation to Europe, by making a selection from a range of alternatives.

Children's images of the world

The children's free-recall maps of the world on both plane and spherical surfaces were analysed and categorised into five model types (Figure 2). These show a strong association with age. The youngest children drew an archipelago of very similar, enclosed 'lands' indicating little understanding of the difference between continents, countries and other places. With increasing age, these became progressively differentiated by size and shape. The first embryonic map elements of correct spatial relationships revealed 'pairings' of countries, such as Great Britain and Ireland, France and Spain, USA and Mexico, China and Japan. By about 7 to 10 years, most children drew maps which indicated an understanding of how places 'nest' inside each other, such as countries within continents. However, even in the later primary years, only 10% of children could make a representation of the world with all seven continents present and in approximately the correct relative location. Africa was the most frequently omitted continent. The location of Australia was clearly recalled in both the map-drawing task and the placing of cut-out shapes. Few children, however, could accurately locate Australia on a globe. This situation was reversed for Antarctica. Whereas most children could locate Antarctica on the globe, few could locate it (perhaps unsurprisingly) on a world map.

Europe and Africa were generally positioned too far south on both map and globe. This seems to have been a result of their (partial and sometimes faulty) knowledge of climate. Knowing that Italy and Spain were warm led many children to place southern Europe near the equator, leaving little room for Africa. As a result, Africa was often positioned 'sideways', a decision supported by the knowledge that 'it was all hot'.

Children's free-recall maps often represent Eurasia as two separate land masses (Figure 3). Reference to a globe may explain why. Whereas the Europe/Africa land area is readily viewed as one integrated unit, the eastern 'edge' of Europe may represent the limit of what can be seen from that same viewpoint. This may be indicative of

Figure 1. Junior school children generally have substantial misconceptions about the configuration of Africa, Australasia and Antarctica

✔ *Generally correct*
✗ *Generally incorrect*

Could children:	Europe	Asia	N. America	S. America	Africa	Australasia	Antarctica
identify the shape?	✔	✔	✔	✔	✗	✗	✗
estimate the size?		✗ under	✔	✔	✔	✗ over	✗ over
locate on a map?	✗	✔	✔	✔	✗	✔	✗
locate on a globe?	✗	✗	✔	✔	✗	✗	✔

the way small-scale spatial information is stored in children's minds (i.e. as smaller 'chunks' of much larger shapes). It is important for teachers to help children get the 'big picture' by seeing how continents stand in relation to each other.

Some shapes on the world map appear to be more memorable than others. The 'boot' of Italy, the Alaskan peninsula, the Panama isthmus, the Iberian peninsula and Cape York/Gulf of Carpentaria were all shown with a consistently high degree of accuracy. Other shapes, seemingly no less obvious, were less well represented, for example, the Florida peninsula.

When it comes to comparing the continents many children underestimated the size of Asia and overestimated the size of Antarctica and Australasia. It is possible that the representation of Antarctica as an enlarged strip at the foot of many maps contributes to this error, although some children noted that 'it gets larger in winter'. Other, non-cartographic factors could also influence perception. It is possible, for example, that the current popular prominence of Australia in the media (for example through television soap operas) contributes to the idea of it being larger in area than it really is (Figure 1).

Implications for teaching

There is some evidence to suggest that children are more familiar with a world map than with a globe. A mental image of the world is more readily fixed in map form because, unlike a globe, all the land masses can be seen at one view. However, every world map has distortions of either shape or area (or both) and the type of projection used influences our image of the size, shape and spatial relations of the continents. It would seem a sensible strategy to use the globe and world map *together* throughout the primary years and beyond.

The problem-solving, interactive nature of the work described here may also be of benefit to young learners. Size, shape recognition and matching games have an important role in learning about small-scale space, particularly if they are played in conjunction with a globe and alternative, contrasting world map projections.

Further reading

Wiegand, P. (1995) 'Young children's freehand maps of the world', *International Research in Geographical and Environmental Education*, 4, 1, pp. 19-28.

Wiegand, P. (1997) 'Children's free recall sketch maps of the world on a spherical surface', *International Research in Geographical and Environmental Education*, 6, 3.

Wiegand, P. and Stiell, B. (1996) 'Children's estimations of the sizes of the continents', *Educational Studies*, 22, 1, pp. 57-68.

Wiegand, P. and Stiell, B. (1996) 'Lost continents? Children's understanding of the location and orientation of the earth's land masses', *Educational Studies*, 22, 3, pp. 383-394.

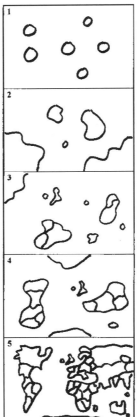

1 Isolated, formless shapes

2 Isolated shapes differentiated by size

3 Land masses divided into areas and becoming more recognisable

4 Land masses distinguished by size, shape and distribution

5 Increasingly accurate representation

Figure 2. Typical sequence of children's free-recall maps of the world

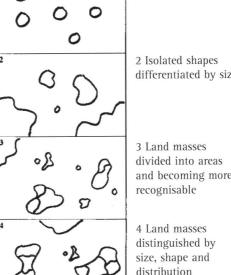

Figure 3. Europe and Asia are commonly drawn as two land masses

Figure 4. Comparing circular world views with a globe

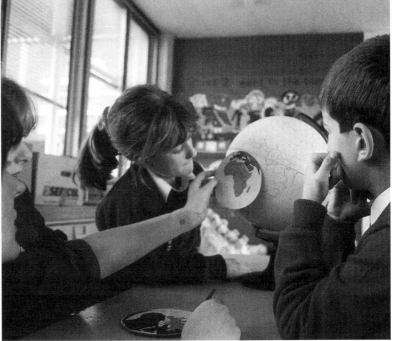

The Way Ahead

Colin Bridge

At the current time there are major questions about assessing learning, raising standards and refining and redefining the geography curriculum. In order to answer them we need to have much clearer objectives and more evidence about how children learn.

In the current educational climate there is a prevailing feeling that theories are fleeting, good practice is a mirage, and the only certainty is constant change. For some, change is invigorating, but for many it produces a great sense of unease.

There are, however, some constants and teachers' own perspectives are grounded in certainties: the school is there each day, the children come in, the timetable demands attention and parents expect some kind of purposeful teaching to take place. In contemplating the day ahead, the most fundamental questions inevitably arise: *What is most useful for the children to learn? How best might I go about teaching it?* and *How can I measure success?* These questions should provide a useful basis for researchers, educationalists and policy makers to work together to provide suggestions for day-to-day practice and mechanisms for evaluation and development.

This is not the place to reflect on why such a goal has not been achieved, but the fact remains that many researchers think it is naive to expect practical outcomes from their work, geographers themselves continue to argue over the nature of geographical enquiry and policy makers have raised the demands of subject disciplines above the needs of learners. Where does this leave the thoughtful primary teacher, for whom there are clear needs and interests? The children they are teaching are in the process of developing spatial awareness in 'real life', but how does this process take place? Teachers need to know this, and they also want to know whether the opportunities they offer the children at various ages are appropriate, and how much and in what way teaching is reflected in understanding.

Although some valuable work has been done to address these questions, much more remains to be done. Research findings appear to have little impact in the classroom and are largely ignored when policy is being formulated. In one way or another, channels need to be established so that key ideas can stretch down through the education system to develop a meaningful pedagogy. The curriculum, as Graves puts it, needs to be both 'practical and theoretical' (Graves, 1996).

Effective teaching

Perhaps because of the lack of clear long-term outcomes, there has been remarkably little assessment of the effectiveness of teaching in primary geography or the quality and depth of children's understanding. This is both worrying and surprising, especially in view of the interest which has been shown in children's level of achievement in science. For example, *Assessing Science in the Primary Classroom* (STAR Project, see Cavendish *et al.*, 1990) and *Science Processes and Concept Formation* (SPACE Project, see Harlen and Black, 1990) are two highly successful research projects. The extent of children's misconceptions in the field of science, and the way teaching must recognise them, is one of the main research stories of the decade.

Geography desperately needs similar in-depth investigations. However, before research into misconceptions and levels of understanding can have any real meaning, greater certainty will be needed about the forms, content and desired outcomes of primary geography.

The ideas proposed by Keith Cooper (1976) still set a standard for any current discussion. Alan Blyth (1990) has brought this discussion forward. He mentions the 'concept ladder' approach for assessing levels of understanding (Gunning, Marsh and Wilson, 1984). This has affinities with the SOLO taxonomy (Biggs and Collis, 1982) developed in Australia. More recently, White and Gunstone (1992) have produced practical strategies for assessing understanding, ranging from 'concept mapping' to 'relational diagrams' and 'question production' (Figure 1).

Looking ahead

Fifteen years ago Michael Naish raised some questions about children's mental development and their learning in geography and observed:

> There is a need for further investigations... concentrating specifically on the skills and concepts involving in geographical study.... Practical programmes of work need to be designed, implemented and evaluated in a continuing effort for curriculum development. *(Naish, 1982)*

I do not believe that this agenda has even begun to be realised. Unfortunately, the geography Order has proved a distraction for primary schools. It has focused attention on the pursuit

Figure 1. Concept mapping has been pioneered as a concise and practical way of exploring children's thinking (after White and Gunstone) (1992)

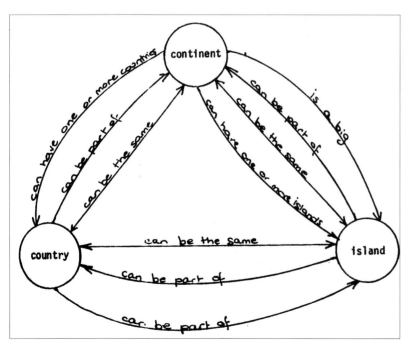

Personal development

Lifeskills
Practical skills (including ICT)
Locational knowledge

Mapwork and wayfinding
Graphicacy
Environmental literacy

Intellectual development

Learning skills, e.g. describing,
explaining and predicting

Key concepts, e.g. change,
pattern and process

Metacognition: transferring concepts
from one context to another

Emotional development

Attachment and belonging
Sense of identity
Sense of place
Caring for the environment
Valuing other people and
cultures

Social development

Using the resources of places
and communities
Responding to current issues

Development education
Trends and lifestyles
Citizenship

Figure 2. How geography can contribute to a curriculum of the future

of factual knowledge which, in the absence of intellectual underpinning, becomes a fruitless chase. In the process we have lost the impetus to investigate an effective pedagogy, we have lost the idea of affective outcomes for the child and we have been distracted from considering what constitutes credible geographical thinking and understanding in young children. There is an urgent need for further research on cognitive development and how to accelerate learning in geography.

At key stages 1 and 2 geography can make a unique contribution to the child's personal, social, intellectual and emotional development. Recent statements from the Geographical Association have highlighted the essential character of the subject and the outcomes that can be achieved in school (Figure 2). This makes an impressive case.

However, now that the millennium review of the National Curriculum is under way, foundation subjects are once again under pressure. There is a danger that this pressure may 'downsize' primary geography or reduce it to a component of an integrated rather than a subject-based curriculum. We must ensure that this does not happen; that the integrity of the subject remains intact; and that children continue to be offered a broad and balanced curriculum in the years ahead.

References and further reading

Biggs, J. and Collis, K. (1982) *Evaluating the Quality of Learning: The SOLO Taxonomy.* London: Academic Press.

Blyth, A. *et al.* (1976) *Curriculum Planning in History, Geography and Social Science.* Bristol: Collins ESL.

Blyth, A. (1990) *Making the Grade for Primary Humanities.* Buckingham: Open University Press.

Cavendish, S. *et al.* (1990) *Assessing Science in the Primary Classroom: Observing Activities.* London: Paul Chapman.

Cooper, K. (1976) *Evaluation, Assessment and Record Keeping in History, Geography and Social Science.* Bristol: Collins ESL.

Galton, M. (1995) *Crisis in the Classroom.* London: David Fulton.

Graves, N. (1996) 'Curriculum development in geography: an ongoing process' in Kent, A. *et al.* (eds) *Geography in Education.* Cambridge: Cambridge University Press, pp. 72-99.

Gunning, D., Marsh, C. and Wilson, J. (1984) *Concept Ladders in School Work.* Trent Papers in Primary School Topic Work 84/2. Nottingham: Trent Polytechnic.

Harlen, W. and Black, P. (1990) *Primary SPACE Project: Research Reports.* Liverpool: Liverpool University Press.

Kaplan, S. (1976) 'Adaption, structure and knowledge' in Moore, G. and Colledge, R. (eds) *Environmental Knowing.* Stroudsburg: Dowden, Hutchinson and Ross, pp. 32-45.

Lynch, K. (1972) *What Time is this Place?* Cambridge Mass.: MIT Press.

Matthews, M. (1992) *Making Sense of Place.* Hemel Hempstead: Harvester Wheatsheaf.

Naish, M. (1982) 'Mental development and the learning of geography' in Graves, R. (ed) *New UNESCO Source Book for Geography Teaching.* Harlow: Longman/UNESCO Press.

Nixon, J. *et al.* (1996) *Encouraging Learning.* Buckingham: Open University Press.

Pick, B. (1977) 'The school as a resource: some suggestions', *Bulletin of Environmental Education,* 76, pp. 4-5.

Scoffham, S., Bridge, C. and Jewson, T. (1986) *Schoolbase Geography.* Huddersfield: Schofield and Sims.

Walmsley, D. and Lewis, G. (1993) *People and Environment.* Harlow: Longman.

White, R. and Gunstone, R. (1992) *Probing Understanding.* London : Falmer Press.

Contributors

Helen Baldwin is a recent BEd graduate of Rolle School of Education, University of Plymouth.

Debbie Bartlett is a landscape manager working in the school grounds consultancy team of Kent Property Services Landscape Department. She also teaches on the BSc landscape management course at the University of Greenwich.

Peter Bloomfield is a senior lecturer in geography and education at the University of Hertfordshire where he works almost exclusively in initial (primary) teacher education. He is a member of the GA Primary and Middle School Section committee and a regular contributor to GA conferences and *Primary Geographer*.

Rachel Bowles lectures in education and environmental studies at the University of Greenwich, Avery Hill Campus. Author of several locality studies, she is editor of the GA Primary Guidance Series and co-ordinator of the Register of Research in Primary Geography (see page 55).

Colin Bridge has worked as a primary school headteacher for many years, is currently Chair of the GA Primary and Middle School Section committee and co-author of several well-known primary geography textbooks.

Simon Catling was a primary teacher for 13 years and is now tutor in primary geography and deputy head of the School of Education, Oxford Brookes University. He has lectured widely on primary geography and mapwork, written extensively for teachers and children and in 1992-3 was president of the GA.

Bill Chambers is head of the Department of Environmental and Biological Studies at Liverpool Hope University College. He has written many primary texts and is a member of the GA Environmental Education Working Group.

Michael Eyres is a recent BEd graduate from Liverpool Hope University College.

Wendy Garner is a lecturer in the Department of Environmental and Biological Studies at Liverpool Hope University College.

John Halocha is lecturer in humanities education in the School of Education, University of Durham. His research and publication activities include the European dimension in education.

Vicki Harrington completed a BA Ed course in primary education at Canterbury Christ Church College in 1995 and is currently researching the rationalisation of primary education in rural areas.

Doug Harwood is a senior lecturer at the University of Warwick. He has published widely in the fields of geographical, political and personal and social education.

Mayer Hillman is Senior Fellow Emeritus of the Policy Studies Institute – Britain's leading independent research organisation undertaking studies of economic and social policy. He has been engaged since 1970 in studies on transport, urban planning, energy conservation, health promotion and environment policies.

Margaret Mackintosh is senior lecturer in primary geography at Rolle School of Education, University of Plymouth and editor of *Primary Geographer*.

Trevelyan May is a recent BEd graduate from Rolle School of Education, University of Plymouth.

Miles Opie is a recent BEd graduate from Rolle School of Education, Exmouth.

Joy Palmer is Dean of the Faculty of Social Sciences, Reader in Education and Director of the Centre for Research on Environmental Thinking and Awareness at the University of Durham. She is Vice-President of the National Association for Environmental Education and a member of the Commission on Education and Communication of the IUCN (the World Conservation Union).

Stephen Scoffham is senior lecturer in primary geography at Canterbury Christ Church College and the author of a variety of textbooks and guides for teachers.

John Sharp is senior lecturer in science and geography education at the University of Plymouth.

Christopher Spencer is Reader in psychology at the University of Sheffield, and in addition to the work on aerial photograph recognition reported here, has also experience of working with blind children and tactile maps; and the use that ten- and twelve-year olds make of their town centres as resources.

Sarah Taylor is a recent BA Ed graduate from Canterbury Christ Church College.

Hugh Ward has a research degree on 'Conceptual thinking in geography' (University of Nottingham MPhil), was appointed General Inspector for primary, middle and secondary schools in Kent in 1978 and served as a member of the Geography National Curriculum Working Group (1989-90) before retiring in 1993.

Steve Watts is senior lecturer in geography education at the University of Sunderland. He has taught in schools for 14 years and was Chair of the GA's Primary and Middle School Section committee 1990-1997.

Patrick Wiegand is senior lecturer in the School of Education at the University of Leeds and well-known for his educational publications and research into children's understanding of maps.

The Register of Research in Primary Geography

This is a directory of teaching and learning observations comprising contributions from several kinds of researchers, as follows:

- People who have developed classroom research on a large scale, e.g. Blyth, Matthews, Spencer and Wiegand.

- Final year and postgraduate students, most of whom produce action research and small-scale investigations.

- Newly qualified teachers (NQTs) and experienced coordinator teachers. This group of practitioners take part, with their classes/school, in investigations of teaching and learning.

- Academics, teacher trainers, local authority advisors and inspectors. Members of this group stimulate and encourage research in the classroom at local, regional and national level.

- Correspondents from overseas (included in the network by courtesy of the IGU Commission on Geographical Education).

The Geographical Association Primary and Middle School Committee has undertaken to care for the Register, which is currently coordinated by Rachel Bowles. The Register is due for publication in 1997/98 and will include an alphabetical classification of correspondents and addresses, cross-referenced to a classification by research interest.

Areas requiring research attention will be listed and a bibliography of key research articles and books given along with a list of Associations with cross-curricular concerns in common with those of geography.

For further information, and enquiries, contact Rachel Bowles, 9 Humber Road, Blackheath, London SE3 7LS.
Tel: 0181 858 5658.
Fax: 0181 858 5685.
E-mail: rabowles@dial.pipex.com

Index

Index by Margaret Binns